Free Video  Free Video

Essential Test Tips Video from Trivium Test Prep

Dear Customer,

Thank you for purchasing from Trivium Test Prep! We're honored to help you prepare for your SAT exam.

To show our appreciation, we're offering a **FREE** *SAT Essential Test Tips* **Video by Trivium Test Prep**.* Our video includes 35 test preparation strategies that will make you successful on the SAT. All we ask is that you email us your feedback and describe your experience with our product. Amazing, awful, or just so-so: we want to hear what you have to say!

To receive your **FREE** *SAT Essential Test Tips* **Video**, please email us at 5star@triviumtestprep.com. Include "Free 5 Star" in the subject line and the following information in your email:

1. The title of the product you purchased.
2. Your rating from 1 – 5 (with 5 being the best).
3. Your feedback about the product, including how our materials helped you meet your goals and ways in which we can improve our products.
4. Your full name and shipping address so we can send your **FREE** *SAT Essential Test Tips* **Video**.

If you have any questions or concerns please feel free to contact us directly at 5star@triviumtestprep.com.

Thank you!

– Trivium Test Prep Team

*To get access to the free video please email us at 5star@triviumtestprep.com, and please follow the instructions above.

SAT Prep Book 2023-2024:
2 Full Practice Tests and SAT Study Guide

Jonathan Cox

Table of Contents

Online Resources

To help you fully prepare for your SAT, Accepted, Inc. includes online resources with the purchase of this study guide.

PRACTICE TESTS

In addition to the practice test included in this book, we also offer an online exam. Since many exams today are computer based, getting to practice your test-taking skills on the computer is a great way to prepare.

FLASH CARDS

A convenient supplement to this study guide, Accepted Inc.'s flash cards enable you to review important terms easily on your computer or smartphone.

CHEAT SHEETS

Review the core skills you need to master the exam with easy-to-read Cheat Sheets.

FROM STRESS to SUCCESS

Watch "From Stress to Success," a brief but insightful YouTube video that offers the tips, tricks, and secrets experts use to score higher on the exam.

REVIEWS

Leave a review, send us helpful feedback, or sign up for Accepted, Inc. promotions—including free books!

Access these materials at:
www.acceptedinc.com/sat-2020-online-resources

Introduction

Congratulations on choosing to take the SAT! By purchasing this book, you've taken the first step toward your college career. This guide will provide you with a detailed overview of the SAT so you know exactly what to expect on test day. We'll take you through all the concepts covered on the test and give you the opportunity to test your knowledge with practice questions. Even if it's been a while since you took a major test, don't worry; we'll make sure you're more than ready!

What is the SAT?

The SAT (Scholastic Aptitude Test) is an achievement test designed to assess what you've learned in school. Universities will look at your SAT score to help determine if you're ready to tackle college-level material. However, your test score won't be the only thing that schools look at; they'll also consider your high school transcript, letters of recommendation, and school activities. So, while the SAT is an important part of your college application, it's only one part of the application process.

What's on the SAT?

The SAT consists of four sections: Reading, Writing and Language, Mathematics, and an optional essay.

The Mathematics section is further broken down into two parts: one that's taken with a calculator and one taken without. You will have a reference sheet with common formulas for each math test.

The Reading and Writing sections include only multiple-choice questions, while the Mathematics section includes multiple-choice and grid-ins (shown below). Each test section has a time limit (as specified in the following table), for a total of 154 questions and three hours of testing. If you choose to take the optional essay, you'll write a short expository essay and the test will be extended by fifty minutes.

What's on the SAT?			
SECTION	**CONCEPTS**	**NUMBER OF QUESTIONS**	**TIME**
Reading	understanding and analyzing nonfiction and fiction passages; interpreting graphs and charts; vocabulary in context	52 questions	65 minutes
Writing and Language	identifying errors in basic grammar, punctuation, usage, and style; rhetorical skills	44 questions	35 minutes
Mathematics	mathematical reasoning and performing calculations using algebra, geometry, and basic statistics	20 questions (without calculator)	25 minutes
		38 questions (with calculator)	55 minutes
Essay (optional)	analyze and discuss the argument in a passage	1 prompt	50 minutes
Total		**154 questions**	**3 hours (+50 minutes with essay)**

How is the SAT Scored?

Each question on the SAT is worth one point. There is no guess penalty, meaning there is no penalty for choosing an incorrect answer. So be sure to guess if you do not know the answer to a question; you might get it right!

Your scores for the Reading Test and the Writing and Language Test will be combined to one quantity called "Evidence-Based Reading and Writing."

The total number of questions you answer correctly is your raw score. This score will then be scaled from 200 – 800. You'll receive a single score between 200 and 800 for Evidence-Based Reading and Writing, and another score for the Mathematics section. So, the combined (or composite) score for all three sections will range from 400 – 1600. The essay is scored separately by two graders on a scale of 1 – 4, for a total score of 2 – 8. Although the essay is optional, some colleges may recommend or require a score for this section.

When you register for the test, you can choose which schools you want to receive your scores; you can also wait until after you receive your scores to have them sent to schools. If you take the test multiple times, you'll also be able to pick the scores from a particular date to send (although you cannot pick individual sections from multiple testing dates).

How is the SAT Administered?

The SAT is a pencil-and-paper test offered at a range of schools and testing centers. The test is offered six times a year, and you must register for the test by the deadline (usually one month before the test date). When registering, you will have to decide whether you want to take the exam with or without the essay. Check with your desired colleges about their application requirements; some institutions prefer or even require the essay section. You can register for the SAT online at https://collegereadiness.collegeboard.org/sat/register. There is no limit on how many times you can take the test.

On the day of your test, arrive early and be sure to bring proper identification and your admission ticket. You are required to put away all personal belongings before the test begins. Cell phones and other electronic, photographic, recording, or listening devices are not permitted in the testing center at all.

You are allowed pencils, erasers, and a four-function or scientific calculator on your desk during the test. Calculators may only be used during the designated mathematics section. A watch that will not sound during the test is also allowed. For more details on what to expect on testing day, refer to the College Board website.

About This Guide

This guide will help you to master the most important test topics and also develop critical test-taking skills. We have built features into our books to prepare you for your tests and increase your score. Along with a detailed summary of the format, content, and scoring of the SAT, we offer an in-depth overview of the content knowledge required to pass the exam. In the review you'll find sidebars that provide interesting information, highlight key concepts, and review content so that you can solidify your understanding of the exam's concepts. You can also test your knowledge with sample questions throughout the text and practice questions that reflect the content and format of the exams. We're pleased you've chosen Accepted, Inc. to be a part of your journey!

PART I
Evidence-Based Reading and Writing

Reading: 52 questions ¦ 65 minutes
Writing: 44 questions ¦ 35 minutes

The Evidence-Based Reading and Writing part of the SAT includes two tests: 1) the Reading test and 2) the Writing and Language test. The Reading Test will include four single passages and one set of paired passages that cover a range of topics. You'll likely see at least one fictional passage and also excerpts from works on science, history, and social studies. Some of these passages will be accompanied by tables or graphs. Each passage or set of passages will be followed by ten or eleven questions that cover the following topics:

- ► the main idea of a passage
- ► the role of supporting details in a passage
- ► adding supporting details to a passage
- ► the structure of a passage
- ► the author's purpose
- ► logical inferences that can be drawn from a passage
- ► comparing passages
- ► vocabulary and figurative language

The Writing and Language Test asseses your knowledge of basic grammar, punctuation, and rhetoric. The test will include four passages with various words, phrases, and sentences underlined. The corresponding questions will ask you to revise the underlined text; you can choose to leave the text as-is or replace it with another option. Topics you'll see on the test include:

- ► matching pronouns with their antecedents
- ► matching verbs with their subjects
- ► ensuring that verbs are in the correct tense
- ► correcting sentence structure
- ► placing sentences logically within the passage
- ► determining if sentences belong within a passage

CHAPTER ONE

Reading

The Main Idea

The main idea of a text is the author's purpose in writing a book, article, story, etc. Being able to identify and understand the main idea is a critical skill necessary to comprehend and appreciate what you're reading.

Consider a political election. A candidate is running for office and plans to deliver a speech asserting her position on tax reform. The topic of the speech—tax reform—is clear to voters, and probably of interest to many. However, imagine that the candidate believes that taxes should be lowered. She is likely to assert this argument in her speech, supporting it with examples proving why lowering taxes would benefit the public and how it could be accomplished. While the topic of the speech would be tax reform, the benefit of lowering taxes would be the main idea. Other candidates may have different perspectives on the topic; they may believe that higher taxes are necessary, or that current taxes are adequate. It is likely that their speeches, while on the same topic of tax reform, would have different main ideas: different arguments likewise supported by different examples. Determining what a speaker, writer, or text is asserting about a specific issue will reveal the MAIN IDEA.

One more quick note: the exam may also ask about a passage's THEME, which is similar to but distinct from its topic. While a TOPIC is usually a specific *person*, *place*, *thing*, or *issue*, the theme is an *idea* or *concept* that the author refers back to frequently. Examples of common themes include ideas like the importance of family, the dangers of technology, and the beauty of nature.

There will be many questions on the exam that require you to differentiate between the topic, theme, and main idea of a passage. Let's look at an example:

QUICK REVIEW
Topic: The subject of the passage.

Theme: An idea or concept the author refers to repeatedly.

Main idea: The argument the writer is making about the topic.

Babe Didrikson Zaharias, one of the most decorated female athletes of the twentieth century, is an inspiration for everyone. Born in 1911 in Beaumont, Texas, Zaharias lived in a time when women were considered second-class to men, but she never let that stop her from becoming a champion. Babe was one of seven children in a poor immigrant family, and was competitive from an early age. As a child she excelled at most things she tried, especially sports, which continued into high school and beyond. After high school, Babe played amateur basketball for two years, and soon after began training in track and field. Despite the fact that women were only allowed to enter in three events, Babe represented the United States in the 1932 Los Angeles Olympics, and won two gold medals and one silver for track and field events.

In the early 1930s, Babe began playing golf which earned her a legacy. The first tournament she entered was a men's only tournament; however she did not make the cut to play. Playing golf as an amateur was the only option for a woman at this time, since there was no professional women's league. Babe played as an amateur for a little over a decade, until she turned pro in 1947 for the Ladies Professional Golf Association (LPGA) of which she was a founding member. During her career as a golfer, Babe won eighty-two tournaments, amateur and professional, including the U.S. Women's Open, All-American Open, and British Women's Open Golf Tournament. In 1953, Babe was diagnosed with cancer, but fourteen weeks later, she played in a tournament. That year she won her third U.S. Women's Open. However by 1955, she didn't have the physicality to compete anymore, and she died of the disease in 1956.

The topic of this passage is obviously Babe Zaharias—the whole passage describes events from her life. Determining the main idea, however, requires a little more analysis. The passage describes Babe Zaharias' life, but the main idea of the paragraph is what it says about her life. To figure out the main idea, consider what the writer is saying about Babe Zaharias. The writer is saying that she's someone to admire—that's the main idea and what unites all the information in the paragraph. Lastly, what might the theme of the passage be? The writer refers to several broad concepts, including never giving up and overcoming the odds, both of which could be themes of the passage.

Two major indicators of the main idea of a paragraph or passage follow below:

▶ It is a general idea; it applies to all the more specific ideas in the passage. Every other sentence in a paragraph should be able to relate in some way to the main idea.

▶ It asserts a specific viewpoint that the author supports with facts, opinions, or other details. In other words, the main idea takes a stand.

EXAMPLE

It's easy to puzzle over the landscapes of our solar system's distant planets—how could we ever know what those far-flung places really look like? However, scientists utilize a number of tools to visualize the surfaces of many planets. The topography of Venus, for example, has been explored by several space probes, including the Russian Venera landers and NASA's Magellan orbiter. These craft used imaging and radar to map the surface of the planet, identifying a whole host of features including volcanoes, craters, and a complex system of channels. Mars has likewise been mapped by space probes, including the famous Mars Rovers, which are automated vehicles that actually landed on the planet's surface. These rovers have been used by NASA and other space agencies to study the geology, climate, and possible biology of the planet.

In addition to these long-range probes, NASA has also used its series of orbiting telescopes to study distant planets. These four massively powerful telescopes include the famous Hubble Space Telescope as well as the Compton Gamma Ray Observatory, Chandra X-Ray Observatory, and the Spitzer Space Telescope. These allow scientists to examine planets using not only visible light but also infrared and near-infrared light, ultraviolet light, x-rays and gamma rays.

Powerful telescopes aren't just found in space: NASA makes use of Earth-bound telescopes as well. Scientists at the National Radio Astronomy Observatory in Charlottesville, VA, have spent decades using radio imaging to build an incredibly detailed portrait of Venus' surface. In fact, Earth-bound telescopes offer a distinct advantage over orbiting telescopes because they allow scientists to capture data from a fixed point, which in turn allows them to effectively compare data collected over a long period of time.

1. Which of the following sentences best describes the main idea of the passage?
   A) It's impossible to know what the surfaces of other planets are really like.
   B) Telescopes are an important tool for scientists studying planets in our solar system.
   C) Venus' surface has many of the same features as the Earth's, including volcanoes, craters, and channels.
   D) Scientists use a variety of advanced technologies to study the surface of the planets in our solar system.

TOPIC and SUMMARY SENTENCES

The main idea of a paragraph usually appears within the topic sentence. The TOPIC SENTENCE introduces the main idea to readers; it indicates not only the topic of a passage, but also the writer's perspective on the topic.

Notice, for example, how the first sentence in the text about Babe Zaharias states the main idea: *Babe Didrikson Zaharias, one of the most decorated female athletes of the twentieth century, is an inspiration for everyone.*

Even though paragraphs generally begin with topic sentences due to their introductory nature, on occasion writers build up to the topic sentence by using supporting details in order to generate interest or build an argument. Be alert for paragraphs when writers do not include a clear topic sentence at all; even without a clear topic sentence, a paragraph will still have a main idea. You may also see a **SUMMARY SENTENCE** at the end of a passage. As its name suggests, this sentence sums up the passage, often by restating the main idea and the author's key evidence supporting it.

EXAMPLE

The Constitution of the United States establishes a series of limits to rein in centralized power. Separation of powers distributes federal authority among three competing branches: the executive, the legislative, and the judicial. Checks and balances allow the branches to check the usurpation of power by any one branch. States' rights are protected under the Constitution from too much encroachment by the federal government. Enumeration of powers names the specific and few powers the federal government has. These four restrictions have helped sustain the American republic for over two centuries.

2. In the above paragraph, what are the topic and summary sentences?

IMPLIED MAIN IDEA

A paragraph without a clear topic sentence still has a main idea; rather than clearly stated, it is implied. Determining the implied main idea requires some detective work: you will need to look at the author's word choice and tone in addition to the content of the passage to find his or her main idea. Let's look at an example paragraph.

EXAMPLES

One of my summer reading books was *Mockingjay*. Though it's several hundred pages long, I read it in just a few days. I was captivated by the adventures of the main character and the complicated plot of the book. However, I felt like the ending didn't reflect the excitement of the story. Given what a powerful personality the main character has, I felt like the ending didn't do her justice.

3. Even without a clear topic sentence, this paragraph has a main idea. What is the writer's perspective on the book—what is the writer saying about it?

A) *Mockingjay* is a terrific novel.

B) *Mockingjay* is disappointing.

C) *Mockingjay* is full of suspense.

D) *Mockingjay* is a lousy novel.

Read the following paragraph:

Fortunately, none of Alyssa's coworkers have ever seen inside the large filing drawer in her desk. Disguised by the meticulous neatness of the rest of her workspace, the drawer betrayed no sign of the chaos within. To even open it, she had to struggle for several minutes with the enormous pile of junk jamming the drawer, until it would suddenly give way, and papers, folders, and candy wrappers spilled out onto the floor. It was an organizational nightmare, with torn notes and spreadsheets haphazardly thrown on top of each other and melted candy smeared across pages. She was worried the odor would soon waft to her coworkers' desks, revealing her secret.

4. Which sentence best describes the main idea of the paragraph above?

A) Alyssa wishes she could move to a new desk.

B) Alyssa wishes she had her own office.

C) Alyssa is glad none of her coworkers know about her messy drawer.

D) Alyssa is sad because she doesn't have any coworkers.

Supporting Details

SUPPORTING DETAILS provide more support for the author's main idea. For instance, in the Babe Zaharias example, the writer makes the general assertion that *Babe Didrikson Zaharias, one of the most decorated female athletes of the twentieth century, is an inspiration for everyone.* The rest of the paragraph provides supporting details with facts showing why she is an inspiration: the names of the challenges she overcame, and the specific years she competed in the Olympics.

Be alert for **SIGNAL WORDS**, which indicate supporting details and so can be helpful in identifying supporting details. Signal words can also help you rule out sentences that are not the main idea or topic sentence: if a sentence begins with one of these phrases, it will likely be too specific to be a main idea.

DID YOU KNOW?
The SAT questions almost always refer to specific lines in the text, so you don't need to read the entire passage before you start answering the questions.

Questions on the SAT will ask you to find details that support a particular idea and also to explain why a particular detail was included in the passage. In order to answer these questions, you must have a solid understanding of the passage's main idea. With this knowledge, you can determine how a supporting detail fits in with the larger structure of the passage.

EXAMPLES

It's easy to puzzle over the landscapes of our solar system's distant planets—how could we ever know what those far-flung places really look like? However, scientists utilize a number of tools to visualize the surfaces of many planets. The topography of Venus, for example, has been explored by several space probes, including the Russian Venera landers and NASA's Magellan orbiter. These craft used imaging and radar to map the surface of the planet, identifying a whole host of features including volcanoes, craters, and a complex system of channels. Mars has likewise been mapped by space probes, including the famous Mars Rovers, which are automated vehicles that actually landed on the planet's surface. These rovers have been used by NASA and other space agencies to study the geology, climate, and possible biology of the planet.

In addition to these long-range probes, NASA has also used its series of orbiting telescopes to study distant planets. These four massively powerful telescopes include the famous Hubble Space Telescope as well as the Compton Gamma Ray Observatory, Chandra X-Ray Observatory, and the Spitzer Space Telescope. These allow scientists to examine planets using not only visible light but also infrared and near-infrared light, ultraviolet light, x-rays and gamma rays.

Powerful telescopes aren't just found in space: NASA makes use of Earth-bound telescopes as well. Scientists at the National Radio Astronomy Observatory in Charlottesville, VA, have spent decades using radio imaging to build an incredibly detailed portrait of Venus' surface. In fact, Earth-bound telescopes offer a distinct advantage over orbiting telescopes because they allow scientists to capture data from a fixed point, which in turn allows them to effectively compare data collected over a long period of time.

5. Which sentence from the text best develops the idea that scientists make use of many different technologies to study the surfaces of other planets?

    A) These rovers have been used by NASA and other space agencies to study the geology, climate, and possible biology of the planet.

    B) It's easy to puzzle over the landscapes of our solar system's distant planets—how could we ever know what those far-flung places really look like?

    C) In addition to these long-range probes, NASA has also used its series of orbiting telescopes to study distant planets.

    D) These craft used imaging and radar to map the surface of the planet, identifying a whole host of features including volcanoes, craters, and a complex system of channels.

6. If true, which sentence could be added to the passage above to support the author's argument that scientists use many different technologies to study the surface of planets?

    A) Because the Earth's atmosphere blocks x-rays, gamma rays, and infrared radiation, NASA needed to put telescopes in orbit above the atmosphere.

    B) In 2015, NASA released a map of Venus which was created by compiling images from orbiting telescopes and long-range space probes.

    C) NASA is currently using the Curiosity and Opportunity rovers to look for signs of ancient life on Mars.

    D) NASA has spent over $2.5 billion to build, launch, and repair the Hubble Space Telescope.

7. The author likely included the detail that Earth-bound telescopes offer a distinct advantage over orbiting telescopes because they allow scientists to capture data from a fixed point in order to

    A) explain why it has taken scientists so long to map the surface of Venus

    B) suggest that Earth-bound telescopes are the most important equipment used by NASA scientists

    C) prove that orbiting telescopes will soon be replaced by Earth-bound telescopes

    D) demonstrate why NASA scientists rely on many different types of scientific equipment

Text Structure

Authors can structure passages in a number of different ways. These distinct organizational patterns, referred to as TEXT STRUCTURE, use the logical relationships between ideas to improve the readability and coherence of a text. The most common ways passages are organized include:

▶ **PROBLEM-SOLUTION:** The author presents a problem and then discusses a solution.

▶ **COMPARE-CONTRAST:** The author presents two situations and then discusses their similarities and differences.

▶ **CAUSE-EFFECT:** The author presents an action and then discusses the resulting effects.

▶ **DESCRIPTIVE:** The author describes an idea, object, person, or other item in detail.

EXAMPLE

The issue of public transportation has begun to haunt the fast-growing cities of the southern United States. Unlike their northern counterparts, cities like Atlanta, Dallas, and Houston have long promoted growth out and not up—these are cities full of sprawling suburbs and single-family homes, not densely concentrated skyscrapers and apartments. What to do then, when all those suburbanites need to get into the central business districts for work? For a long time it seemed highways were the twenty-lane wide expanses of concrete that would allow commuters to move from home to work and back again. But these modern miracles have become time-sucking, pollution-spewing nightmares. They may not like it, but it's time for these cities to turn toward public transport like trains and buses if they are to remain livable.

8. The organization of this passage can best be described as:

   A) a comparison of two similar ideas

   B) a description of a place

   C) a discussion of several effects all related to the same cause

   D) a discussion of a problem followed by the suggestion of a solution

The Author's Purpose

Whenever an author writes a text, she always has a purpose, whether that's to entertain, inform, explain, or persuade. A short story, for example, is meant to entertain, while an online news article would be designed to inform the public about a current event. Each of these different types of writing has a specific name:

▶ **NARRATIVE WRITING** tells a story. (novel, short story, play)

▶ **EXPOSITORY WRITING** informs people. (newspaper and magazine articles)

▶ **TECHNICAL WRITING** explains something. (product manual, directions)

▶ **PERSUASIVE WRITING** tries to convince the reader of something. (opinion column on a blog)

On the exam, you may be asked to categorize a passage as one of these types, either by specifically naming it as such or by identifying its general purpose.

DID YOU KNOW?
When reading, pay attention to characters and people, their titles, dates, places, main ideas, quotations, and italics. Don't be afraid to underline or circle important points in the text.

You may also be asked about primary and secondary sources. These terms describe not the writing itself but the author's relationship to what's being written about. A **PRIMARY SOURCE** is an unaltered piece of writing that was composed during the time when the events being described took place; these texts are often written by the people directly involved. A **SECONDARY SOURCE** might address the same topic but provide extra commentary or analysis. These texts are written by outside observers and may even be composed after the event. For example, a book written by a political candidate to inform people about his or her stand on an issue is a primary source. An online article written by a journalist analyzing how that position will affect the election is a secondary source; a book by a historian about that election would be a secondary source, too.

EXAMPLE

Elizabeth closed her eyes and braced herself on the armrests that divided her from her fellow passengers. Take-off was always the worst part for her. The revving of the engines, the way her stomach dropped as the plane lurched upward; it made her feel sick. Then, she had to watch the world fade away beneath her, getting smaller and smaller until it was just her and the clouds hurtling through the sky. Sometimes (but only sometimes) it just had to be endured, though. She focused on the thought of her sister's smiling face and her new baby nephew as the plane slowly pulled onto the runway.

9. This passage is reflective of which type of writing?
   A) narrative
   B) expository
   C) technical
   D) persuasive

Facts vs. Opinions

On the SAT you might be asked to identify a statement in a passage as either a fact or an opinion, so you'll need to know the difference between the two. A FACT is a statement or thought that can be proven to be true. The statement *Wednesday comes after Tuesday* is a fact—you can point to a calendar to prove it. In contrast, an OPINION is an assumption that is not based in fact and cannot be proven to be true. The assertion that television is more entertaining than feature films is an opinion—people will disagree on this, and there's no reference you can use to prove or disprove it.

DID YOU KNOW?
Keep an eye out for answer choices that may be facts, but which are not stated or discussed in the passage.

EXAMPLE

Exercise is critical for healthy development in children. Today, there is an epidemic of unhealthy children in the United States who will face health problems in adulthood due to poor diet and lack of exercise in childhood. This is a problem for all Americans, especially with the rising cost of health care.

It is vital that school systems and parents encourage their children to engage in a minimum of thirty minutes of cardiovascular exercise each day, mildly increasing their heart rate for a sustained period. This is proven to decrease the likelihood of developmental diabetes, obesity, and a multitude of other health problems. Also, children need a proper diet rich in fruits and vegetables so that they can grow and develop physically, as well as learn healthy eating habits early on.

10. Which of the following is a fact in the passage, not an opinion?
    A) Fruits and vegetables are the best way to help children be healthy.
    B) Children today are lazier than they were in previous generations.
    C) The risk of diabetes in children is reduced by physical activity.
    D) Children should engage in thirty minutes of exercise a day.

Drawing Conclusions

In addition to understanding the main idea and factual content of a passage, you'll also be asked to take your analysis one step further and anticipate what other information could logically be added to the passage. In a non-fiction passage, for example, you might be asked which statement the author of the passage would agree with. In an excerpt from a fictional work, you might be asked to anticipate what a character would do next.

To answer these questions, you must have a solid understanding of the topic, theme, and main idea of the passage; armed with this information, you can figure out which of the answer choices best fits within those criteria (or alternatively, which ones do not). For example, if the author of the passage is advocating for safer working conditions in textile factories, any supporting details that would be added to the passage should support that idea. You might add sentences that contain information about the number of accidents that occur in textile factories or that outline a new plan for fire safety.

EXAMPLES

Today, there is an epidemic of unhealthy children in the United States who will face health problems in adulthood due to poor diet and lack of exercise during their childhoods. This is a problem for all Americans, as adults with chronic health issues are adding to the rising cost of healthcare. A child who grows up living an unhealthy lifestyle is likely to become an adult who does the same.

Because exercise is critical for healthy development in children, it is vital that school systems and parents encourage their children to engage in a minimum of thirty minutes of cardiovascular exercise each day. Even this small amount of exercise has been proven to decrease the likelihood that young people will develop diabetes, obesity, and other health issues as adults. In addition to exercise, children need a proper diet rich in fruits and vegetables so that they can grow and develop physically. Starting a good diet early also teaches children healthy eating habits they will carry into adulthood.

11. The author of this passage would most likely agree with which statement?
    A) Parents are solely responsible for the health of their children.
    B) Children who do not want to exercise should not be made to.
    C) Improved childhood nutrition will help lower the amount Americans spend on healthcare.
    D) It's not important to teach children healthy eating habits because they will learn them as adults.

Elizabeth closed her eyes and braced herself on the armrests that divided her from her fellow passengers. Take-off was always the worst part for her. The revving of the engines, the way her stomach dropped as the plane lurched upward; it made her feel sick. Then, she had to watch the world fade away beneath her, getting smaller and smaller until it was just her and the clouds hurtling through the sky. Sometimes (but only sometimes) it just had to be endured, though. She focused on the thought of her sister's smiling face and her new baby nephew as the plane slowly pulled onto the runway.

12. Which of the following is Elizabeth least likely to do in the future?

    A) Take a flight to her brother's wedding.

    B) Apply for a job as a flight attendant.

    C) Never board an airplane again.

    D) Get sick on an airplane.

Meaning of Words and Phrases

On the Reading section you may be asked to provide definitions or intended meanings for words within passages. You may have never encountered some of these words before the test, but there are tricks you can use to figure out what they mean.

CONTEXT CLUES

A fundamental vocabulary skill is using context to determine the meaning of a word. There are two types of context that can help you understand unfamiliar words: situational context and sentence context. Regardless of which context you encounter, these types of questions are not really testing your knowledge of vocabulary; rather, they test your ability to comprehend the meaning of a word through its usage.

SITUATIONAL CONTEXT helps you determine the meaning of a word through the setting or circumstances in which that word or phrase occurs. Using **SENTENCE CONTEXT** requires analyzing only the sentence in which the new word appears to understand it. To figure out words using sentence context clues, you should first identify the most important words in the sentence.

There are four types of clues that can help you understand the context, and therefore the meaning of a word:

▶ **RESTATEMENT CLUES** occur when the definition of the word is clearly stated in the sentence.

▶ **POSITIVE/NEGATIVE CLUES** can tell you whether a word has a positive or negative meaning.

▶ **CONTRAST CLUES** include the opposite meaning of a word. Words like *but, on the other hand*, and *however* are tip-offs that a sentence contains a contrast clue.

▶ **SPECIFIC DETAIL CLUES** provide a precise detail that can help you understand the meaning of the word.

It is important to remember that more than one of these clues can be present in the same sentence. The more there are, the easier it will be to determine the meaning of the word. For example, the following sentence uses both restatement and positive/negative clues: *Janet suddenly found herself destitute, so poor she could barely afford to eat.* The second part of the sentence clearly indicates that destitute is a negative word. It also restates the meaning: very poor.

EXAMPLES

13. I had a hard time reading her <u>illegible</u> handwriting.
   A) neat
   B) unsafe
   C) sloppy
   D) educated

14 The dog was <u>dauntless</u> in the face of danger, braving the fire to save the girl trapped inside the building.
   A) difficult
   B) fearless
   C) imaginative
   D) startled

15. Beth did not spend any time preparing for the test, but Tyrone kept a <u>rigorous</u> study schedule.
   A) strict
   B) loose
   C) boring
   D) strange

ANALYZING WORDS

As you no doubt know, determining the meaning of a word can be more complicated than just looking in a dictionary. A word might have more than one **DENOTATION**, or definition; which one the author intends can only be judged by examining the surrounding text. For example, the word *quack* can refer to the sound a duck makes, or to a person who publicly pretends to have a qualification which he or she does not actually possess.

A word may also have different **CONNOTATIONS**, which are the implied meanings and emotions a word evokes in the reader. For example, a cubicle is simply a walled desk in an office, but for many the word implies a constrictive, uninspiring workplace. Connotations can vary greatly between cultures and even between individuals.

Lastly, authors might make use of **FIGURATIVE LANGUAGE**, which is the use of a word to imply something other than the word's literal definition. This is often done by comparing two things. If you say *I felt like a butterfly when I got a new haircut*, the listener knows you don't resemble an insect but instead felt beautiful and transformed.

WORD STRUCTURE

Although you are not expected to know every word in the English language for the SAT, you can use deductive reasoning to determine the answer choice that is the best match for the word in question by breaking down unfamiliar vocabulary. Many complex words can be broken down into three main parts:

PREFIX — ROOT — SUFFIX

ROOTS are the building blocks of all words. Every word is either a root itself or has a root. Just as a plant cannot grow without roots, neither can vocabulary, because a word must have a root to give it meaning. The root is what is left when you strip away all the prefixes and suffixes from a word. For example, in the word *unclear*, if you take away the prefix *un-*, you have the root *clear*.

Roots are not always recognizable words; they generally come from Latin or Greek words like *nat*, a Latin root meaning *born*. The word *native*, which describes a person born in a referenced place, comes from this root, as does the word *prenatal*, meaning before birth. It's important to keep in mind, however, that roots do not always match the exact definitions of words, and they can have several different spellings.

Prefixes are syllables added to the beginning of a word, and suffixes are syllables added to the end of the word. Both carry assigned meanings and can be attached to a word to completely change the word's meaning or to enhance the word's original meaning.

Take the word *prefix* itself as an example: *fix* means to place something securely, and *pre-* means before. Therefore, *prefix* means to place something before or in front of. Now let's look at a suffix: in the word *portable*, *port* is a root which means to move or carry. The suffix *-able* means that something is possible. Thus, *portable* describes something that can be moved or carried.

Although you cannot determine the meaning of a word by a prefix or suffix alone, you can use this knowledge to eliminate answer choices; understanding whether the word is positive or negative can give you the partial meaning of the word.

Comparing Passages

In addition to analyzing single passages, the SAT will also require you to compare two passages. Usually these passages will discuss the same topic, and it will be your task to identify the similarities and differences between the authors' main ideas, supporting details, and tones.

EXAMPLES

Read Passages One and Two, and then answer questions 16 and 17.

Passage One

Today, there is an epidemic of unhealthy children in the United States who will face health problems in adulthood due to poor diet and lack of exercise during their childhoods: in 2012, the Centers for Disease Control found that 18 percent of students aged 6-11 were obese. This is a problem for all Americans, as adults with chronic health issues are adding to the rising cost of healthcare. A child who grows up living an unhealthy lifestyle is likely to become an adult who does the same.

Because exercise is critical for healthy development in children, it is vital that school systems and parents encourage their children to engage in a minimum of thirty minutes of cardiovascular exercise each day. Even this small amount of exercise has been proven to decrease the likelihood that young people will develop diabetes, obesity, and other health issues as adults. In addition to exercise, children need a proper diet rich in fruits and vegetables so that they can grow and develop physically. Starting a good diet early also teaches children healthy eating habits they will carry into adulthood.

Passage Two

When was the last time you took a good, hard look at a school lunch? For many adults, it's probably been years—decades even—since they last thought about students' midday meals. If they did stop to ponder, they might picture something reasonably wholesome if not very exciting: a peanut butter and jelly sandwich paired with an apple, or a traditional plate of meat, potatoes, and veggies. At worst, they may think, kids are making due with some pizza and a carton of milk.

The truth, though, is that many students aren't even getting the meager nutrients offered up by a simple slice of pizza. Instead, schools are serving up heaping helpings of previously frozen, recently fried delicacies like french fries and chicken nuggets. These high-carb, low-protein options are usually paired with a limp, flavorless, straight-from-the-freezer vegetable that quickly gets tossed in the trash. And that carton of milk? It's probably a sugar-filled chocolate sludge, or it's been replaced with a student's favorite high-calorie soda.

So what, you might ask. Kids like to eat junk food—it's a habit they'll grow out of soon enough. Besides, parents can always pack lunches for students looking for something better. But is that really the lesson we want to be teaching our kids? Many of those children aren't going to grow out of bad habits; they're going to reach adulthood thinking that ketchup is a vegetable. And students in low-income families are particularly impacted by the sad state of school food. These parents rely on schools to provide a warm, nutritious meal because they don't have the time or money to prepare food at home. Do we really want to be punishing these children with soggy meat patties and salt-soaked potato chips?

16. Both authors are arguing for the importance of improving childhood nutrition. How do the authors' strategies differ?

   A) Passage 1 presents several competing viewpoints while Passage 2 offers a single argument.

   B) Passage 1 uses scientific data while Passage 2 uses figurative language.

   C) Passage 1 is descriptive while Passage 2 uses a cause-effect structure.

   D) Passage 1 has a friendly tone while the tone of Passage 2 is angry.

17. Both authors argue that

   A) children should learn healthy eating habits at a young age.

   B) low-income students are disproportionately affected by the low-quality food offered in schools.

   C) teaching children about good nutrition will lower their chances of developing diabetes as adults.

   D) schools should provide children an opportunity to exercise every day.

Answer Key

1. A) can be eliminated because it directly contradicts the rest of the passage, which goes into detail about how scientists have learned about the surfaces of other planets. Answers B) and C) can also be eliminated because they offer only specific details from the passage; while both choices contain details from the passage, neither is general enough to encompass the passage as a whole. **Only answer D) provides an assertion that is both supported by the passage's content and general enough to cover the entire passage.**

2. **The topic sentence is the first sentence in the paragraph.** It introduces the topic of discussion, in this case the constitutional limits on centralized power. The summary sentence is the last sentence in the paragraph. It sums up the information that was just presented: here, that constitutional limits have helped sustain the United States of America for over two hundred years.

3. **B) is correct**: the novel is disappointing. The process of elimination will reveal the correct answer if that is not immediately clear. While the paragraph begins with positive commentary on the book—*I was captivated by the adventures of the main character and the complicated plot of the book*—this positive idea is followed by the contradictory transition word *however*. A) cannot be the correct answer because the author concludes that the novel was poor. Likewise, D) cannot be correct because it does not encompass all the ideas in the paragraph; despite the negative conclusion, the author enjoyed most of the book. The main idea should be able to encompass all of the thoughts in a paragraph; choice D) does not apply to the beginning of this paragraph. Finally, choice C) is too specific; it could only apply to the brief description of the plot and adventures of the main character. That leaves choice B) as the best option. The author initially enjoyed the book, but was disappointed by the ending, which seemed unworthy of the exciting plot and character.

4. Clearly, Alyssa has a messy drawer, and **C) is the right answer**. The paragraph begins by indicating her gratitude that her coworkers do not know about her drawer (*Fortunately, none of Alyssa's coworkers have ever seen inside the large filing drawer in her desk*). Plus, notice how the drawer is described: *it was an organizational nightmare*, and it apparently doesn't even function properly: *to even open the drawer, she had to struggle for several minutes...* The writer reveals that it even has an odor, with old candy inside.

    Alyssa is clearly ashamed of her drawer and fearful of being judged by her coworkers about it.

5. You're looking for details from the passage that supports the main idea—scientists make use of many different technologies to study the surfaces of other planets. Answer A) includes a specific detail about rovers, but does not offer any details that support the idea of multiple technologies being used. Similarly, answer D) provides another specific detail about space probes. Answer B) doesn't provide any supporting details; it simply introduces the topic of the passage. **Only answer C) provides a detail that directly supports**

the author's assertion that scientists use multiple technologies to study the planets.

6. You can eliminate answers C) and D) because they don't address the topic of studying the surface of planets. Answer A) can also be eliminated because it only addresses a single technology. **Only choice B) would add support to the author's claim about the importance of using multiple technologies.**

7. **Only answer D) relates directly to the author's main argument.** The author doesn't mention how long it has taken to map the surface of Venus (answer A), nor does he say that one technology is more important than the others (answer B). And while this detail does highlight the advantages of using Earth-bound telescopes, the author's argument is that many technologies are being used at the same time, so there's no reason to think that orbiting telescopes will be replaced (answer C).

8. You can exclude answer choice C) because the author provides no root cause or a list of effects. From there this question gets tricky, because the passage contains structures similar to those described above. For example, it compares two things (cities in the North and South) and describes a place (a sprawling city). However, if you look at the overall organization of the passage, you can see that it starts by presenting a problem (transportation) and then presents a solution (trains and buses), making **answer D) the only choice that encompasses the entire passage**.

9. The passage is telling a story—we meet Elizabeth and learn about her fear of flying—so **it's a narrative text, answer choice A)**. There is no factual information presented or explained, nor is the author trying to persuade the reader of anything.

10. Choice B) can be discarded immediately because it is negative (recall that particularly negative answer statements are generally wrong) and is not discussed anywhere in the passage. Answers A) and D) are both opinions—the author is promoting exercise, fruits, and vegetables as a way to make children healthy. (Notice that these incorrect answers contain words that hint at being an opinion such as best, should, or other comparisons.) **Answer C), on the other hand, is a simple fact stated by the author**; it appears in the passage with the word *proven*, indicating that you don't just need to take the author's word for it.

11. **The author would most likely support answer C)**: he mentions in the first paragraph that poor diets are adding to the rising cost of healthcare. The main idea of the passage is that nutrition and exercise are important for children, so answer B) doesn't make sense—the author would likely support measures to encourage children to exercise. Answers A) and D) can also be eliminated because they are directly contradicted in the text. The author specifically mentions the role of school systems, so he doesn't believe parents are solely responsible for their children's health. He also specifically states that children

who grow up with unhealthy eating habits will become adults with unhealthy eating habits, which contradicts D).

12. It's clear from the passage that Elizabeth hates flying, but is willing to endure it for the sake of visiting her family. Thus, it seems likely that she would be willing to get on a plane for her brother's wedding, making A) and C) incorrect answers. The passage also explicitly tells us that she feels sick on planes, so D) is likely to happen. We can infer, though, that she would not enjoy being on an airplane for work, so she's very unlikely to apply for a job as a flight attendant, which is **choice B)**.

13. Already, you know that this sentence is discussing something that is hard to read. Look at the word that illegible is describing: handwriting. Based on context clues, you can tell that illegible means that her handwriting is hard to read.

   Next, look at the answer choices. Choice A), *neat*, is obviously a wrong answer because neat handwriting would not be difficult to read. Choices B) and D), *unsafe* and *educated*, don't make sense. Therefore, **choice C), *sloppy*, is the best answer**.

14. **Demonstrating bravery in the face of danger would be B), fearless.** In this case, the restatement clue (*braving the fire*) tells you exactly what the word means.

15. In this case, the contrast word *but* tells us that Tyrone studied in a different way than Beth, which means it's a contrast clue. If Beth did not study hard, then Tyrone did. **The best answer, therefore, is choice A).**

16. The first author uses scientific facts (*the Centers for Disease Control found...* and *Even this small amount of exercise has been proven...*) to back up his argument, while the second uses figurative language (the *ironic delicacies* and the metaphor *sugar-filled chocolate sludge*), so **the correct answer is B)**. Answer A) is incorrect because the first author does not present any opposing viewpoints. Answer C) is incorrect because Passage 2 does not have a cause-effect structure. And while the author of the second passage could be described as angry, the first author is not particularly friendly, so you can eliminate answer D) as well.

17. **Both authors argue children should learn healthy eating habits at a young age (answer A).** The author of Passage 1 states that a child who grows up living an unhealthy lifestyle is likely to become an adult who does the same, and the author of Passage 2 states that many of those children aren't going to grow out of bad habits—both of these sentences argue that it's necessary to teach children about nutrition early in life. Answers C) and D) are mentioned only by the author of Passage 1, and answer B) is only discussed in Passage 2.

CHAPTER TWO
Writing and Language

Parts of Speech

The first step in getting ready for the Writing and Language Test is to review parts of speech and the rules that accompany them. The good news is that you have been using these rules since you first began to speak; even if you don't know a lot of the technical terms, many of these rules may be familiar to you.

DID YOU KNOW?
Remember that you can write on the test booklet—cross out wrong answer choices and other parts of the text you may find confusing.

NOUNS and PRONOUNS

NOUNS are people, places, or things. For example, in the sentence *The hospital was very clean*, the noun is hospital; it is a place. Pronouns replace nouns and make sentences sound less repetitive. Take the sentence *Sam stayed home from school because Sam was not feeling well*. The word *Sam* appears twice in the same sentence. To avoid repetition and improve the sentence, use a pronoun instead: *Sam stayed at home because he did not feel well*.

Because pronouns take the place of nouns, they need to agree both in number and gender with the noun they replace. So, a plural noun needs a plural pronoun, and a feminine noun needs a feminine pronoun. In the first sentence of this paragraph, for example, the plural pronoun *they* replaced the plural noun *pronouns*. There will usually be several questions on the SAT Writing and Language Test that cover pronoun agreement, so it's good to get comfortable spotting pronouns.

QUICK REVIEW
Singular pronouns:
▶ I, me, mine, my
▶ you, your, yours
▶ he, him, his
▶ she, her, hers
▶ it, its

Plural pronouns:
▶ we, us, our, ours
▶ they, them, their, theirs

EXAMPLES

1. Which sentence below is correct?
    A) If a student forgets their homework, it is considered incomplete.
    B) If a student forgets his or her homework, it is considered incomplete.

2. Which sentence below is correct?
    A) Everybody will receive their paychecks promptly.
    B) Everybody will receive his or her paycheck promptly.

3. Which sentence below is correct?
    A) When a nurse begins work at a hospital, you should wash your hands.
    B) When a nurse begins work at a hospital, he or she should wash his or her hands.

4. Which sentence below is correct?
    A) After the teacher spoke to the student, she realized her mistake.
    B) After Mr. White spoke to his student, she realized her mistake. (she and her referring to student)
    C) After speaking to the student, the teacher realized her own mistake. (her referring to teacher)

VERBS

A **VERB** is the action of a sentence: verbs *do* things. A verb must be conjugated to match the context of the sentence; this can sometimes be tricky because English has many irregular verbs. For example, *run* is an action verb in the present tense that becomes *ran* in the past tense; the linking verb *is* (which describes a state of being) becomes *was* in the past tense.

Table 2.1. Conjugation of the Verb *To Be*			
	PAST	PRESENT	FUTURE
singular	was	is	will be
plural	were	are	will be

Verb tense must make sense in the context of the sentence. For example, the sentence *I was baking cookies and eat some dough* probably sounds strange. That's because the two verbs *was baking* and *eat* are in different tenses. *Was baking* occurred in the past; *eat*, on the other hand, occurs in the present. To correct this error, conjugate *eat* in the past tense: *I was baking cookies and ate some dough.*

Like pronouns, verbs must agree in number with the noun they refer back to. In the example above, the verb *was* refers back to the singular *I*. If the subject of the sentence was plural, it would need to be modified to read *They were baking cookies and ate some dough*. Note that the verb *ate* does not change form; this is common for verbs in the past tense.

QUICK REVIEW
If the subject is separated from the verb, cross out the phrases between them to make conjugation easier.

EXAMPLES

5. Which sentence below is correct?
   A) The cat chase the ball while the dogs runs in the yard.
   B) The cat chases the ball while the dogs run in the yard.

6. Which sentence below is correct?
   A) The cars that had been recalled by the manufacturer was returned within a few months.
   B) The cars that had been recalled by the manufacturer were returned within a few months.

7. Which sentence below is correct?
   A) The deer hid in the trees.
   B) The deer are not all the same size.

8. Which sentence below is correct?
   A) The doctor and nurse work in the hospital.
   B) Neither the nurse nor her boss was scheduled to take a vacation.
   C) Either the patient or her parents complete her discharge paperwork.

9. Which sentence below is correct?
   A) Because it will rain during the party last night, we had to move the tables inside.
   B) Because it rained during the party last night, we had to move the tables inside.

ADJECTIVES and ADVERBS

ADJECTIVES are words that describe a noun. Take the sentence *The boy hit the ball*. If you want to know more about the noun *ball*, then you could use an adjective to describe him: *The boy hit the red ball*. An adjective simply provides more information about a noun in a sentence.

Like adjectives, **ADVERBS** provide more information about a part of a sentence. Adverbs can describe verbs, adjectives, and even other adverbs. For example, in the sentence

The doctor had recently hired a new employee, the adverb *recently* tells us more about how the action *hired* took place. Often, but not always, adverbs end in *–ly*. Remember that adverbs can never describe nouns—only adjectives can.

Adjectives, adverbs, and *modifying phrases* (groups of words that together modify another word) should always be placed as close as possible to the word they modify. Separating words from their modifiers can result in incorrect or confusing sentences.

EXAMPLES

10. Which sentence below is correct?

    A) Running through the hall, the bell rang and the student knew she was late.

    B) Running through the hall, the student heard the bell ring and knew she was late.

11. Which sentence below is correct?

    A) The terrifyingly lion's loud roar scared the zoo's visitors.

    B) The lion's terrifyingly loud roar scared the zoo's visitors.

OTHER PARTS of SPEECH

PREPOSITIONS generally help describe relationships in space and time; they may express the location of a noun or pronoun in relation to other words and phrases in a sentence. For example, in the sentence *The nurse parked her car in a parking garage*, the preposition *in* describes the position of the car in relation to the garage. The noun that follows the preposition is called its *object*. In the example above, the object of the preposition *in* is the noun *parking garage*.

DID YOU KNOW?
Just a few other prepositions include *after, between, by, during, of, on, to,* and *with.*

CONJUNCTIONS connect words, phrases, and clauses. The conjunctions summarized in the acronym FANBOYS—for, and, nor, but, or, yet, so—are called **COORDINATING CONJUNCTIONS** and are used to join independent clauses. For example, in the sentence *The nurse prepared the patient for surgery, and the doctor performed the surgery*, the conjunction *and* joins the two independent clauses together. **SUBORDINATING CONJUNCTIONS**, like *although, because,* and *if,* join together an independent and dependent clause. In the sentence *She had to ride the subway because her car was broken*, the conjunction *because* joins together the two clauses. (Independent and dependent clauses are covered in more detail below.)

QUICK REVIEW
See *Phrases and Clauses* for more on independent and dependent clauses.

INTERJECTIONS, like *wow* and *hey*, express emotion and are most commonly used in conversation and casual writing. They are often followed by *exclamation points*.

Constructing Sentences
PHRASES and CLAUSES

A **PHRASE** is a group of words acting together that contain either a subject or verb, but not both. Phrases can be constructed from several different parts of speech. For example, a prepositional phrase includes a preposition and the object of that preposition (e.g., *under the table*), and a verb phrase includes the main verb and any helping verbs (e.g., *had been running*). Phrases cannot stand alone as sentences.

A **CLAUSE** is a group of words that contains both a subject and a verb. There are two types of clauses: **INDEPENDENT CLAUSES** can stand alone as sentences, and **DEPENDENT CLAUSES** cannot stand alone. Again, dependent clauses are recognizable as they begin with subordinating conjunctions.

EXAMPLE

12. Classify each of the following as a phrase, independent clause, or dependent clause:

1) I have always wanted to drive a bright red sports car

2) under the bright sky filled with stars

3) because my sister is running late

TYPES of SENTENCES

A sentence can be classified as simple, compound, complex, or compound-complex based on the type and number of clauses it has.

Table 2.2. Sentence Classification		
SENTENCE TYPE	NUMBER OF INDEPENDENT CLAUSES	NUMBER OF DEPENDENT CLAUSES
simple	1	0
compound	2+	0
complex	1	1+
compound-complex	2+	1+

A **SIMPLE SENTENCE** consists of only one independent clause. Because there are no dependent clauses in a simple sentence, it can be as short as two words, a subject and a verb (e.g., *I ran.*). However, a simple sentence may also contain prepositions, adjectives, and adverbs. Even though these additions can extend the length of a simple sentence, it is still considered a simple sentence as long as it doesn't contain any dependent clauses.

COMPOUND SENTENCES have two or more independent clauses and no dependent clauses. Usually a comma and a coordinating conjunction (*for, and, nor, but, or, yet,* and *so*) join the independent clauses, though semicolons can be used as well. For example, the sentence *My computer broke, so I took it to be repaired* is compound.

DID YOU KNOW?
Joining two independent clauses with only a comma and no coordinating conjunction is a punctuation error called a comma splice—be on the lookout for these.

COMPLEX SENTENCES have one independent clause and at least one dependent clause. In the complex sentence *If you lie down with dogs, you'll wake up with fleas,* the first clause is dependent (because of the subordinating conjunction *if*), and the second is independent.

COMPOUND-COMPLEX SENTENCES have two or more independent clauses and at least one dependent clause. For example, the sentence *City traffic frustrates David because the streets are congested, so he is seeking an alternate route home,* is compound-complex. *City traffic frustrates David* is an independent clause, as is *he is seeking an alternate route home*; however the subordinating conjunction *because* indicates that *because the streets are so congested* is a dependent clause.

EXAMPLES

13. Classify the following sentence: *San Francisco is one of my favorite places in the United States.*
    A) A simple sentence
    B) A compound sentence
    C) A complex sentence
    D) A compound-complex sentence

14. Classify the following sentence: *I love listening to the radio in the car because I enjoy loud music on the open road.*
    A) A simple sentence
    B) A compound sentence
    C) A complex sentence
    D) A compound-complex sentence

15. Classify the following sentence: *I wanted to get a dog, but I got a fish because my roommate is allergic to pet dander.*
    A) A simple sentence
    B) A compound sentence
    C) A complex sentence
    D) A compound-complex sentence

16. Classify the following sentence: *The game was canceled, but we will still practice on Saturday.*

    A) A simple sentence

    B) A compound sentence

    C) A complex sentence

    D) A compound-complex sentence

CLAUSE PLACEMENT

In addition to the classifications above, sentences can also be defined by the location of the main clause. In a periodic sentence, the main idea of the sentence is held until the end. In a cumulative sentence, the independent clause comes first, and any modifying words or clauses follow it. (Note that this type of classification—periodic or cumulative—is not used in place of the simple, compound, complex, or compound-complex classifications. A sentence can be both cumulative and complex, for example.)

EXAMPLES

17. Classify the following sentence: *The GED, the TASC, the SAT, the ACT—this dizzying array of exams proved no match for the determined students.*

    A) A cumulative sentence

    B) A periodic sentence

18. Classify the following sentence: *Jessica was well prepared for the test, for she had studied for weeks, taken practice exams, and reviewed the material with other students.*

    A) A cumulative sentence

    B) A periodic sentence

Punctuation

The basic rules for using the major punctuation marks are given in Table 2.3.

Table 2.3. Basic Punctuation Rules		
PUNCTUATION	PURPOSE	EXAMPLE
period	ending sentences	Periods go at the end of complete sentences.
question mark	ending questions	What's the best way to end a sentence?

Table 2.3. Basic Punctuation Rules (continued)

PUNCTUATION	PURPOSE	EXAMPLE
exclamation point	indicating interjections or commands; ending sentences that show extreme emotion	Help! I'll never understand how to use punctuation!
comma	joining two independent clauses (always with a coordinating conjunction)	Commas can be used to join independent clauses, but they must always be followed by a coordinating conjunction in order to avoid a comma splice.
	setting apart introductory and nonessential words and phrases	Commas, when used properly, set apart extra information in a sentence.
	separating three or more items in a list	My favorite punctuation marks include the colon, semicolon, and period.
semicolon	joining together two independent clauses (never with a conjunction)	I love semicolons; they make sentences so concise!
colon	introducing a list, explanation, or definition	When I see a colon I know what to expect: more information.
apostrophe	form contractions	It's amazing how many people can't use apostrophes correctly.
	show possession	The students' grammar books are out of date, but the school's principal cannot order new ones yet.
quotation marks	indicate a direct quote	I said to her, "Tell me more about parentheses."

EXAMPLES

19. Which sentence below is correct?

A) Her roommate asked her to pick up milk, and a watermelon from the grocery store.

B) Her roommate asked her to pick up milk and a watermelon from the grocery store.

20. Which sentence below is correct?

A) The softball coach—who had been in the job for only a year, quit unexpectedly on Friday.

B) The softball coach—who had been in the job for only a year—quit unexpectedly on Friday.

C) The softball coach, who had been in the job for only a year, quit unexpectedly on Friday

21. Which sentence below is correct?

A) I'd like to order a hamburger, with extra cheese, but my friend says I should get a fruit salad instead.

B) I'd like to order a hamburger with extra cheese, but my friend says I should get a fruit salad instead.

Point of View

A sentence's **POINT OF VIEW** is the perspective from which it is written. Point of view is described as either first, second, or third person.

Table 2.4. Point of View			
PERSON	PRONOUNS	WHO'S ACTING?	EXAMPLE
first	I, we	the writer	I take my time when shopping for shoes.
second	you	the reader	You prefer to shop online.
third	he, she, it, they	the subject	She buys shoes from her cousin's store.

First person perspective appears when the writer's personal experiences, feelings, and opinions are an important element of the text. Second person perspective is used when the author directly addresses the reader. Third person perspective is most common in formal and academic writing; it creates distance between the writer and the reader. A sentence's point of view must remain consistent.

EXAMPLE

22. Which sentence below is correct?

A) If someone wants to be a professional athlete, you have to practice often.

B) If you want to be a professional athlete, you have to practice often.

C) If someone wants to be a professional athlete, he or she has to practice often.

Active and Passive Voice

Sentences can be written in active voice or passive voice. **ACTIVE VOICE** means that the subjects of the sentences are performing the action of the sentence. In a sentence written in **PASSIVE VOICE**, the subjects are being acted on. The sentence *Justin wrecked my car* is in the active voice because the subject (*Justin*) is doing the action (*wrecked*). The sentence can be rewritten in passive voice by using a *to be* verb: *My car was wrecked by Justin.* Now the subject of the sentence (*car*) is being acted on. It's also possible to write the sentence so that the person performing the action is not identified: *My car was wrecked.*

Generally, good writing will avoid using passive voice. However, when it is unclear who or what performed the action of the sentence, passive voice may be the only option.

EXAMPLES

23. Rewrite the following sentence in active voice: *I was hit with a stick by my brother.*

24. Rewrite the following sentence in passive voice: *My roommate made coffee this morning.*

Transitions

TRANSITIONS connect two ideas and also explain the logical relationship between them. For example, the transition *because* tells you that two things have a cause and effect relationship, while the transitional phrase *on the other hand* introduces a contradictory idea. On the SAT Writing and Language Test you may be asked to identify the best transition for a particular sentence, and you will definitely need to make good use of transitions in your essay.

DID YOU KNOW?
Don't be afraid to choose "No Change"—it will be the correct choice around a quarter of the time!

Table 2.5. Common Transitions	
CAUSE AND EFFECT	AS A RESULT, BECAUSE, CONSEQUENTLY, DUE TO, IF/THEN, SO, THEREFORE, THUS
Similarity	also, likewise, similar, between
Contrast	but, however, in contrast, on the other hand, nevertheless, on the contrary, yet
Concluding	briefly, finally, in conclusion, in summary, to conclude
Addition	additionally, also, as well, further, furthermore, in addition, moreover
Examples	in other words, for example, for instance, to illustrate
Time	after, before, currently, later, recently, since, subsequently, then, while

EXAMPLES

Choose the transition word or words that would best fit in the blank.

25. Clara's car breaks down frequently. _____, she decided to buy a new one.

A) However

B) For example

C) While

D) Therefore

26. Chad scored more points than any other player on his team. _____, he is often late to practice, so his coach won't let him play in the game Saturday.

A) However

B) For example

C) While

D) Therefore

27. Miguel will often eat his lunch outside. _____, on Wednesday he took his sandwich to the park across from his office.

A) However

B) For example

C) While

D) Therefore

28. Alex set the table _____ the lasagna finished baking in the oven.

A) however

B) for example

C) while

D) therefore

Wordiness and Redundancy

Sometimes sentences can be grammatically correct but still be confusing or poorly written. Often this problem arises when sentences are wordy or contain redundant phrasing (i.e., when several words with similar meanings are used). Often such phrases are used to make the writing seem more serious or academic when actually they can confuse the reader. On the test, you might be asked to clarify or even remove such phrases.

Some examples of excessive wordiness and redundancy include:

- I'll meet you in the *place where I parked my car.* → I'll meet you in the *parking lot.*

- *The point I am trying to make is that* the study was flawed. → The study was flawed.

- A memo was sent out *concerning the matter of* dishes left in the sink. → A memo was sent out *about* dishes left in the sink.

- The email was *brief and to the point.* → The email was *terse.*

- I don't think I'll ever *understand or comprehend* Italian operas. → I don't think I'll ever *understand* Italian operas.

EXAMPLES

Rewrite each of the following sentences to eliminate wordiness and redundancy.

29. The game was canceled due to the fact that a bad storm was predicted.

30. The possibility exists that we will have a party for my mother's birthday.

31. With the exception of our new puppy, all of our dogs have received their vaccinations.

32. We threw away the broken microwave that didn't work.

33. It was an unexpected surprise when we won the raffle.

Answer Key

1. **B) is correct.** *Student* is a singular noun, but *their* is a plural pronoun, making the first sentence grammatically incorrect. To correct it, replace *their* with the singular pronoun *his* or *her*.

2. **B) is correct.** *Everybody* is a singular noun, but *their* is a plural pronoun; the first sentence is grammatically incorrect. To correct it, replace *their* with the singular pronoun *his* or *her*.

3. **B) is correct.** This sentence begins in third-person perspective and finishes in second-person perspective. To correct it, ensure the sentence finishes with third-person perspective.

4. **B) and C) are correct.** This sentence refers to a teacher and a student. But to whom does *she* refer, the teacher or the student? To improve clarity, use specific names or state more clearly who spotted the mistake.

5. **B) is correct.** *Cat* is singular, so it takes a singular verb (which confusingly ends with an s); *dogs* is plural, so it needs a plural verb.

6. **B) is correct.** Sometimes the subject and verb are separated by clauses or phrases. Here, the subject *cars* is separated from the verb phrase *were returned*, making it more difficult to conjugate the verb correctly; this results in a number error.

7. **A) and B) are correct.** The subject of these sentences is a collective noun, which describes a group of people or things. This noun can be singular if it is referring to the group as a whole or plural if it refers to each item in the group as a separate entity.

8. **A), B), and C) are correct.** When the subject contains two or more nouns connected by *and*, that subject is plural and requires a plural verb. Singular subjects joined by *or, either/or, neither/nor,* or *not only/but also* remain singular; when these words join plural and singular subjects, the verb should match the closest subject.

9. **B) is correct.** All the verb tenses in a sentence need to agree both with each other and with the other information in the sentence. In the first sentence, the tense doesn't match the other information in the sentence: *last night* indicates the past (rained) not the future (will rain).

10. **B) is correct.** The phrase *running through the hall* should be placed next to *student*, the noun it modifies.

11. **B) is correct.** While the lion may indeed be terrifying, the word *terrifyingly* is an adverb and so can only modify a verb, an adjective or another adverb, not the noun *lion*. In the second sentence, *terrifyingly* is modifying the adjective *loud*, telling us more about the loudness of the lion's roar—so loud, it was terrifying.

12. **1 is an independent clause—it** has a subject (*I*) and a verb (*have*

wanted) and has no subordinating conjunction. **2 is a phrase** made up of a preposition (*under*), its object (*sky*), and words that modify sky (*bright, filled with stars*), but lacks a conjugated verb. **3 is a dependent clause**—it has a subject (*sister*), a verb (*is running*), and a subordinating conjunction (*because*).

13. **A) is correct.** Although the sentence is lengthy, it is simple because it contains only one subject and verb (*San Francisco... is*) modified by additional phrases.

14. **C) is correct.** The sentence has one independent clause (*I love... car*) and one dependent (*because I... road*), so it is complex.

15. **D) is correct.** This sentence has three clauses: two independent (*I wanted... dog* and *I got a fish*) and one dependent (*because my... dander*), so it is compound-complex.

16. **B) is correct.** This sentence is made up of two independent clauses joined by a conjunction (*but*), so it is compound.

17. **B) is correct.** In this sentence the main independent clause—*this... students*—is held until the very end, so it's periodic. Furthermore, despite its length the sentence is simple because it has only one subject (*dizzying array*) and verb (*proved*).

18. **A) is correct.** Here, the main clause *Jessica...test* begins the sentence; the other clauses modify the main clause, providing more information about the main idea and resulting in a

cumulative sentence. In addition, the sentence is compound as it links two independent clauses together with a comma and the coordinating conjunction *for*.

19. **B) is correct.** Commas are only needed when joining three items in a series; this sentence only has two (milk and watermelon).

20. **B) and C) are correct.** When setting apart nonessential words and phrases, you can use either dashes or commas, but not both.

21. **B) is correct.** Prepositional phrases are usually essential to the meaning of the sentence, so they don't need to be set apart with commas. Here, the prepositional phrase *with extra cheese* helps the reader understand that the speaker wants a particularly unhealthy meal; however, the friend is encouraging a healthier option. Removing the prepositional phrase would limit the contrast between the burger and the salad. Note that the second comma remains because it is separating two independent clauses.

22. **B) and C) are correct.** In the first sentence, the person shifts from third (*someone*) to second (*you*). It needs to be rewritten to be consistent.

23. First, identify the person or object performing the action (usually given in a prepositional phrase— here, *by my brother*) and make it the subject; the subject of the original sentence (*I*) becomes the object. Remove the *to be* verb: *My brother hit me with a stick.*

24. Here, the object (*coffee*) becomes the subject; move the original subject (*my roommate*) to a prepositional phrase at the end of the sentence. Add the *to be* verb: *The coffee was made this morning by my roommate.*

25. **D) is correct.** The sentence is describing a cause (*her car breaks down*) and an effect (*she'll buy a new one*), so the correct transition is *therefore*.

26. **A) is correct.** The sentence includes a contrast: it would make sense for Chad to play in the game, but he isn't, so the best transition is *however*.

27. **B) is correct.** In the sentence, the clause after the transition is an example, so the best transition is *for example*.

28. **C) is correct.** In the sentence, two things are occurring at the same time, so the best transition is *while*.

29. The game was canceled because a bad storm was predicted.

    Replace the long phrase *due to the fact that* with the much shorter *because*.

30. We might have a party for my mother's birthday.

    By rearranging the sentence, we can replace the phrase *the possibility exists that* with the word *might*.

31. All of our dogs have been vaccinated except our new puppy.

    The sentence can be rearranged to replace *with the exception of* with *except*. The phrase *receive their vaccinations* has also been shortened to *been vaccinated*.

32. We threw away the broken microwave.

    If something is broken that means it doesn't work, so the phrase *that didn't work* can be removed.

33. It was a surprise when we won the raffle.

    By definition, a surprise is always unexpected, so the word *unexpected* can be removed.

PART II
Mathematics

20 questions ¦ 25 minutes (without calculator)

38 questions ¦ 55 minutes (with calculator)

The Mathematics section of the SAT tests your knowledge of math concepts taught through the tenth grade, including geometry, algebra, statistics, probability, and trigonometry. The majority of the questions will require you to use complex reasoning to work through multiple steps—you won't simply be performing calculations. Instead, you can expect to perform tasks like building equations from word problems, comparing expressions, and interpreting figures.

The first twenty questions of the Mathematics section have to be done without a calculator; you may use a calculator on the final thirty-eight questions. You can use any calculator that can't access the internet, including graphing calculators. Note that you cannot use the calculator on your tablet or phone.

There are two types of questions on the Mathematics section: multiple-choice and grid-in. For the grid-in questions, you will be required to provide an answer—no answer choices will be provided for you. A couple of notes about grid-in answers:

▶ Answers cannot be given as mixed numbers—you must convert the answer to a decimal or improper fraction.

▶ Decimal numbers must be rounded to fit in the grid. Do not include the zero before the decimal point; instead you can place the decimal point in the left-most column.

▶ There are no negative answers on the grid-in questions.

▶ You will only receive credit for answers that are bubbled in; you will NOT get credit if you only write the answer in the box at the top of the grid.

CHAPTER THREE

Numbers and Operations

In order to do any type of math—whether it's basic geometry or advanced calculus—you need to have a solid understanding of numbers and operations. The specific operations the SAT will test you on are covered in this chapter. However, we won't be covering basic arithmetic operations like adding fractions or long division, since you'll be able to perform these on your calculator during the test.

Types of Numbers

INTEGERS are whole numbers, including the counting numbers, the negative counting numbers and zero. 3, 2, 1, 0, –1, –2, –3 are examples of integers. RATIONAL NUMBERS are made by dividing one integer by another integer. They can be expressed as fractions or as decimals. Three divided by 4 makes the rational number $\frac{3}{4}$ or 0.75. IRRATIONAL NUMBERS are numbers that cannot be written as fractions; they are decimals that go on forever without repeating. The number π (3.14159...) is an example of an irrational number.

Imaginary numbers are numbers that, when squared, give a negative result. Imaginary numbers use the symbol i to represent $\sqrt{-1}$, so $3i = 3\sqrt{-1}$ and $(3i)^2 = -9$. COMPLEX NUMBERS are combinations of real and imaginary numbers, written in the form $a + bi$, where a is the real number and bi is the imaginary number. An example of a complex number is $4 + 2i$. When adding complex numbers, add the real and imaginary numbers separately: $(4 + 2i) + (3 + i) = 7 + 3i$.

1. Is $\sqrt{5}$ a rational or irrational number?

2. What kind of number is $-\sqrt{64}$?

3. Solve: $(3 + 5i) - (1 - 2i)$

Working with Positive and Negative Numbers

Adding, multiplying, and dividing numbers can yield positive or negative values depending on the signs of the original numbers. Knowing these rules can help determine if your answer is correct.

(+) + (−) = the sign of the larger number

(−) + (−) = negative number

(−) × (−) = positive number

(−) × (+) = negative number

(−) ÷ (−) = positive number

(−) ÷ (+) = negative number

EXAMPLES

4. Find the product of −10 and 47.

5. What is the sum of −65 and −32?

6. Is the product of −7 and 4 less than −7, between −7 and 4, or greater than 4?

7. What is the value of −16 divided by 2.5?

Order of Operations

Operations in a mathematical expression are always performed in a specific order, which is described by the acronym PEMDAS:

1. Parentheses

2. Exponents

3. Multiplication

4. Division

5. Addition

6. Subtraction

Perform the operations within parentheses first, and then address any exponents. After those steps, perform all multiplication and division. These are carried out from left to right as they appear in the problem. Finally, do all required addition and subtraction, also from left to right as each operation appears in the problem.

EXAMPLES

8. Solve: $[-(2)^2 - (4 + 7)]$

9. Solve: $(5)^2 \div 5 + 4 \times 2$

10. Solve the expression: $15 \times (4 + 8) - 3^3$

11. Solve the expression: $\left(\frac{5}{2} \times 4\right) + 23 - 4^2$

Units of Measurement

You are expected to memorize some units of measurement. These are given below. When doing unit conversion problems (i.e., when converting one unit to another), find the conversion factor, then apply that factor to the given measurement to find the new units.

Table 3.1. Unit Prefixes		
PREFIX	SYMBOL	MULTIPLICATION FACTOR
tera	T	1,000,000,000,000
giga	G	1,000,000,000
mega	M	1,000,000
kilo	k	1,000
hecto	h	100
deca	da	10
base unit	--	--
deci	d	0.1
centi	c	0.01
milli	m	0.001
micro	µ	0.0000001
nano	n	0.0000000001
pico	p	0.0000000000001

Table 3.2. Units and Conversion Factors

Dimension	American	SI
length	inch/foot/yard/mile	meter
mass	ounce/pound/ton	gram
volume	cup/pint/quart/gallon	liter
force	pound-force	newton
pressure	pound-force per square inch	pascal
work and energy	cal/British thermal unit	joule
temperature	Fahrenheit	kelvin
charge	faraday	coulomb

Conversion Factors

1 in = 2.54 cm
1 yd = 0.914 m
1 mile = 1.61 km
1 gallon = 3.785 L
1 oz = 28.35 g

1 lb = 0.454 kg
1 cal = 4.19 J
$1 \,°F = \frac{5}{9}(°F - 32)$
$1 \,cm^3 = 1 \,mL$
1 hour = 3600 s

EXAMPLES

12. A fence measures 15 ft. long. How many yards long is the fence?

13. A pitcher can hold 24 cups. How many gallons can it hold?

14. A spool of wire holds 144 in. of wire. If Mario has 3 spools, how many feet of wire does he have?

15. A ball rolling across a table travels 6 inches per second. How many feet will it travel in 1 minute?

16. How many millimeters are in 0.5 meters?

17. A lead ball weighs 38 g. How many kilograms does it weigh?

18 How many cubic centimeters are in 10 L?

19. Jennifer's pencil was initially 10 centimeters long. After she sharpened it, it was 9.6 centimeters long. How many millimeters did she lose from her pencil by sharpening it?

Decimals and Fractions
ADDING and SUBTRACTING DECIMALS

When adding and subtracting decimals, line up the numbers so that the decimals are aligned. You want to subtract the ones place from the ones place, the tenths place from the tenths place, and so on.

EXAMPLES

20. Find the sum of 17.07 and 2.52.

21. Jeannette has 7.4 gallons of gas in her tank. After driving, she has 6.8 gallons. How many gallons of gas did she use?

MULTIPLYING and DIVIDING DECIMALS

When multiplying decimals, start by multiplying the numbers normally. You can then determine the placement of the decimal point in the result by adding the number of digits after the decimal in each of the numbers you multiplied together.

When dividing decimals, you should move the decimal point in the divisor (the number you're dividing by) until it is a whole number. You can then move the decimal in the dividend (the number you're dividing into) the same number of places in the same direction. Finally, divide the new numbers normally to get the correct answer.

EXAMPLES

22. What is the product of 0.25 and 1.4?

23. Find $0.8 \div 0.2$.

24. Find the quotient when 40 is divided by 0.25.

WORKING with FRACTIONS

FRACTIONS are made up of two parts: the NUMERATOR, which appears above the bar, and the DENOMINATOR, which is below it. If a fraction is in its SIMPLEST FORM, the numerator and the denominator share no common factors. A fraction with a numerator larger than its denominator is an IMPROPER FRACTION; when the denominator is larger, it's a PROPER FRACTION.

Improper fractions can be converted into proper fractions by dividing the numerator by the denominator. The resulting whole number is placed to the left of the fraction, and the remainder becomes the new numerator; the denominator does not change. The new number is called a **MIXED NUMBER** because it contains a whole number and a fraction. Mixed numbers can be turned into improper fractions through the reverse process: multiply the whole number by the denominator and add the numerator to get the new numerator.

EXAMPLES

25. Simplify the fraction $\frac{121}{77}$.

26. Convert $\frac{37}{5}$ into a proper fraction.

MULTIPLYING and DIVIDING FRACTIONS

To multiply fractions, convert any mixed numbers into improper fractions and multiply the numerators together and the denominators together. Reduce to lowest terms if needed.

To divide fractions, first convert any mixed fractions into single fractions. Then, invert the second fraction so that the denominator and numerator are switched. Finally, multiply the numerators together and the denominators together.

DID YOU KNOW?
Inverting a fraction changes multiplication to division:
$$\frac{a}{b} \div \frac{c}{d} = \frac{a}{b} \times \frac{d}{c} = \frac{ad}{bc}$$

EXAMPLES

27. Find $\frac{7}{8} \div \frac{1}{4}$.

28. What is the product of $\frac{1}{12}$ and $\frac{6}{8}$?

29. Find the quotient: $\frac{2}{5} \div 1\frac{1}{5}$.

30. A recipe calls for $\frac{1}{4}$ cup of sugar. If 8.5 batches of the recipe are needed, how many cups of sugar will be used?

ADDING and SUBTRACTING FRACTIONS

Adding and subtracting fractions requires a **COMMON DENOMINATOR**. To find the common denominator, you can multiply each fraction by the number 1. With fractions, any number over itself (e.g., $\frac{5}{5}$, $\frac{12}{12}$) is equivalent to 1, so multiplying by such a fraction can change the denominator without changing the value of the fraction. Once the denominators are the same, the numerators can be added or subtracted.

DID YOU KNOW?
The phrase *simplify the expression* just means you need to perform all the operations in the expression.

To add mixed numbers, first add the whole numbers and then the fractions. To subtract mixed numbers, convert each number to an improper fraction, then subtract the numerators.

EXAMPLES

31. Simplify the expression: $\frac{2}{3} - \frac{1}{5}$.

32. Find $2\frac{1}{3} - \frac{3}{2}$.

33. Find the sum of $\frac{9}{16}$, $\frac{1}{2}$, and $\frac{7}{4}$.

34. Sabrina has $\frac{2}{3}$ of a can of red paint. Her friend Amos has $\frac{1}{6}$ of a can. How much red paint do they have combined?

CONVERTING FRACTIONS to DECIMALS

Calculators are not allowed on a portion of the SAT, which can make handling fractions and decimals intimidating for many test takers. However, there are several helpful techniques you can use to navigate between the two forms.

The first thing to do is simply memorize common decimals and their fractional equivalents; a list of these is given below. With these values, it's possible to convert more complicated fractions as well. For example, $\frac{2}{5}$ is just $\frac{1}{5}$ multiplied by 2, so $\frac{2}{5} = 0.2 \times 2 = 0.4$.

Table 3.3. Fractions to Decimals	
FRACTION	DECIMAL
$\frac{1}{2}$	0.5
$\frac{1}{3}$	$0.\overline{33}$
$\frac{1}{4}$	0.25
$\frac{1}{5}$	0.2
$\frac{1}{6}$	$0.1\overline{66}$
$\frac{1}{7}$	$0.\overline{142857}$
$\frac{1}{8}$	0.125
$\frac{1}{9}$	$0.\overline{11}$
$\frac{1}{10}$	0.1

Knowledge of common decimal equivalents to fractions can also help you estimate. This skill can be particularly helpful on multiple-choice tests like the SAT, where excluding incorrect answers is just as helpful as knowing how to find the right one. For example, to find $\frac{5}{8}$ in decimal form for an answer, you can eliminate any answers less than 0.5 because $\frac{4}{8}$ = 0.5. You may also know that $\frac{6}{8}$ is the same as $\frac{3}{4}$ or 0.75, so anything above 0.75 can be eliminated as well.

Another helpful trick is to check if the denominator is easily divisible by 100; for example in the fraction $\frac{9}{20}$, you know 20 goes into 100 five times, so you can multiply the top and bottom by 5 to get $\frac{45}{100}$ or 0.45.

If none of these techniques work, you'll need to find the decimal by dividing the denominator by the numerator using long division.

EXAMPLES

35. Write $\frac{8}{18}$ as a decimal.

36. Write the fraction $\frac{3}{16}$ as a decimal.

CONVERTING DECIMALS to FRACTIONS

Converting a decimal into a fraction is more straightforward than the reverse process is. To convert a decimal, simply use the numbers that come after the decimal as the numerator in the fraction. The denominator will be a power of 10 that matches the place value for the original decimal. For example, the denominator for 0.46 would be 100 because the last number is in the hundredths place; likewise, the denominator for 0.657 would be 1000 because the last number is in the thousandths place. Once this fraction has been set up, all that's left is to simplify it.

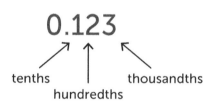

Figure 3.1. Decimal Places

EXAMPLE

37. Convert 0.45 into a fraction.

Ratios

A ratio describes the quantity of one thing in relation to the quantity of another. Unlike fractions, ratios do not give a part relative to a whole; instead, they compare two values. For example, if you have 3 apples and 4 oranges, the ratio of apples to oranges is 3 to 4. Ratios can be written using words (3 to 4), fractions $\left(\frac{3}{4}\right)$, or colons (3:4).

It's helpful to rewrite a ratio as a fraction expressing a part to a whole. For instance, in the example above you have 7 total pieces of fruit, so the fraction of your fruit that is apples is $\frac{3}{7}$, while oranges make up $\frac{4}{7}$ of your fruit collection.

When working with ratios, always consider the units of the values being compared. On the SAT, you may be asked to rewrite a ratio using the same units on both sides. For example, you might have to rewrite the ratio 3 minutes to 7 seconds as 180 seconds to 7 seconds.

EXAMPLES

38. There are 90 voters in a room, and each is either a Democrat or a Republican. The ratio of Democrats to Republicans is 5:4. How many Republicans are there?

39. The ratio of students to teachers in a school is 15:1. If there are 38 teachers, how many students attend the school?

Proportions

A proportion is an equation that equates two ratios. Proportions are usually written as two fractions joined by an equal sign $\left(\frac{a}{b} = \frac{c}{d}\right)$, but they can also be written using colons (a:b::c:d). Note that in a proportion, the units must be the same in both numerators and in both denominators.

Often you will be given three of the values in a proportion and asked to find the fourth. In these types of problems, you can solve for the missing variable by cross-multiplying—multiply the numerator of each fraction by the denominator of the other to get an equation with no fractions as shown below. You can then solve the equation using basic algebra. (For more on solving basic equations, see *Algebraic Expressions*.)

$$\frac{a}{b} = \frac{c}{d} \rightarrow ad = bc$$

EXAMPLES

40. A train traveling 120 miles takes 3 hours to get to its destination. How long will it take for the train to travel 180 miles?

41. One acre of wheat requires 500 gallons of water. How many acres can be watered with 2600 gallons?

42. If 35:5::49:x, find x.

Percentages

A percent is the ratio of a part to the whole. Questions may give the part and the whole and ask for the percent, or give the percent and the whole and ask for the part, or give the part and the percent and ask for the value of the whole. The equation for percentages can be rearranged to solve for any of these:

$$\text{percent} = \frac{\text{part}}{\text{whole}}$$

$$\text{part} = \text{whole} \times \text{percent}$$

$$\text{whole} = \frac{\text{part}}{\text{percent}}$$

In the equations above, the percent should always be expressed as a decimal. In order to convert a decimal into a percentage value, simply multiply it by 100. So, if you've read 5 pages (the part) of a 10-page article (the whole), you've read $\frac{5}{10}$ = .50 or 50%. (The percent sign (%) is used once the decimal has been multiplied by 100.)

Note that when solving these problems, the units for the part and the whole should be the same. If you're reading a book, saying you've read 5 pages out of 15 chapters doesn't make any sense.

EXAMPLES

43. 45 is 15% of what number?

44. Jim spent 30% of his paycheck at the fair. He spent $15 for a hat, $30 for a shirt, and $20 playing games. How much was his check? (Round to the nearest dollar.)

45. What percent of 65 is 39?

46. Greta and Max sell cable subscriptions. In a given month, Greta sells 45 subscriptions and Max sells 51. If 240 total subscriptions were sold in that month, what percent were not sold by Greta or Max?

47. Grant needs to score 75% on an exam. If the exam has 45 questions, at least how many does he need to answer correctly to get this score?

PERCENT CHANGE

Percent change problems ask you to calculate how much a given quantity has changed. The problems are solved in a similar way to regular percent problems, except that instead of using the *part* you'll use the *amount of change*. Note that the sign of the *amount of change* is important: if the original amount has increased the change will be positive; if it has decreased the change will be negative. Again, in the equations below the percent is a decimal value; you need to multiply by 100 to get the actual percentage.

$$\text{percent change} = \frac{\text{amount of change}}{\text{original amount}}$$

$$\text{amount of change} = \text{original amount} \times \text{percent change}$$

$$\text{original amount} = \frac{\text{amount of change}}{\text{percent change}}$$

EXAMPLES

48. A computer software retailer marks up its games by 40% above the wholesale price when it sells them to customers. Find the price of a game for a customer if the game costs the retailer $25.

49. A golf shop pays its wholesaler $40 for a certain club, and then sells it to a golfer for $75. What is the markup rate?

50. A shoe store charges a 40% markup on the shoes it sells. How much did the store pay for a pair of shoes purchased by a customer for $63?

51. An item originally priced at $55 is marked 25% off. What is the sale price?

52. James wants to put an 18 foot by 51 foot garden in his backyard. If he does, it will reduce the size of his yard by 24%. What will be the area of the remaining yard space?

Comparison of Rational Numbers

Number comparison problems present numbers in different formats and ask which is larger or smaller, or whether the numbers are equivalent. The important step in solving these problems is to convert the numbers to the same format so that it is easier to compare them. If numbers are given in the same format, or after converting them, determine which number is smaller or if the numbers are equal. Remember that for negative numbers, higher numbers are actually smaller.

EXAMPLES

53. Is $4\frac{3}{4}$ greater than, equal to, or less than $\frac{18}{4}$?

54. Which of the following numbers has the greatest value: 104.56, 104.5, or 104.6?

55. Is 65% greater than, less than, or equal to $\frac{13}{20}$?

Exponents and Radicals

Exponents tell us how many times to multiply a base number by itself. In the example 2^4, 2 is the base number and 4 is the exponent. $2^4 = 2 \times 2 \times 2 \times 2 = 16$. Exponents are also called powers: 5 to the third power = $5^3 = 5 \times 5 \times 5 = 125$. Some exponents have special names: x to the second power is also called "x squared" and x to the third power is also called "x cubed." The number 3 squared = $3^2 = 3 \times 3 = 9$.

Radicals are expressions that use roots. Radicals are written in the form $\sqrt[a]{x}$ where a = the **RADICAL POWER** and x = **THE RADICAND**. The solution to the radical $\sqrt[3]{8}$ is the number that, when multiplied by itself 3 times, equals 8. $\sqrt[3]{8} = 2$ because $2 \times 2 \times 2 = 8$. When the radical power is not written we assume it is 2, so $\sqrt{9} = 3$ because $3 \times 3 = 9$. Radicals can also be written as exponents, where the power is a fraction. For example, $x^{\frac{1}{3}} = \sqrt[3]{x}$.

Review more of the rules for working with exponents and radicals in the table below.

Table 3.4. Exponents and Radicals Rules	
RULE	**EXAMPLE**
$x^0 = 1$	$5^0 = 1$
$x^1 = x$	$5^1 = 5$
$x^a \times x^b = x^{a+b}$	$5^2 \times 5^3 = 5^5 = 3125$
$(xy)^a = x^a y^a$	$(5 \times 6)^2 = 5^2 \times 6^2 = 900$
$(x^a)^b = x^{ab}$	$(5^2)^3 = 5^6 = 15{,}625$
$\left(\dfrac{x}{y}\right)^a = \dfrac{x^a}{y^a}$	$\left(\dfrac{5}{6}\right)^2 = \dfrac{5^2}{6^2} = \dfrac{25}{36}$
$\dfrac{x^a}{x^b} = x^{a-b}$ $(x \neq 0)$	$\dfrac{5^4}{5^3} = 5^1 = 5$
$x^{-a} = \dfrac{1}{x^a}$ $(x \neq 0)$	$5^{-2} = \dfrac{1}{5^2} = \dfrac{1}{25}$
$x^{\frac{1}{a}} = \sqrt[a]{x}$	$25^{\frac{1}{2}} = \sqrt[2]{25} = 5$
$\sqrt[a]{x \times y} = \sqrt[a]{x} \times \sqrt[a]{y}$	$\sqrt[3]{8 \times 27} = \sqrt[3]{8} \times \sqrt[3]{27} = 2 \times 3 = 6$
$\sqrt[a]{\dfrac{x}{y}} = \dfrac{\sqrt[a]{x}}{\sqrt[a]{y}}$	$\sqrt[3]{\dfrac{27}{8}} = \dfrac{\sqrt[3]{27}}{\sqrt[3]{8}} = \dfrac{3}{2}$
$\sqrt[a]{x^b} = x^{\frac{b}{a}}$	$\sqrt[2]{5^4} = 5^{\frac{4}{2}} = 5^2 = 25$

EXAMPLES

56. Simplify the expression $2^4 \times 2^2$

57. Simplify the expression $(3^4)^{-1}$

58. Simplify the expression $\left(\dfrac{9}{4}\right)^{\frac{1}{2}}$

Matrices

A **MATRIX** is an array of numbers aligned into horizontal rows and vertical columns. A matrix is described by the number of rows (m) and columns (n) it contains. For example, a matrix with 3 rows and 4 columns is a 3×4 matrix, as shown below.

$$\begin{bmatrix} 2 & -3 & 5 & 0 \\ 4 & -6 & 2 & 11 \\ 3.5 & 7 & 2.78 & -1.2 \end{bmatrix}$$

To add or subtract 2 matrices, simply add or subtract the corresponding numbers in each matrix. Only matrices with the same dimensions can be added or subtracted, and the resulting matrix will also have the same dimensions.

In order to multiply 2 matrices, the number of columns in the first must equal the number of rows in the second. To multiply the matrices, multiply the numbers in each row of the first by the numbers in the column of the second and add. The resulting matrix will have the same number of rows as the first matrix and same number of columns as the second. Note that the order of the matrices is important when they're being multiplied: **AB** is not the same as **BA**.

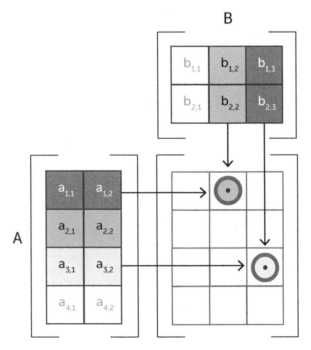

Figure 3.2. Matrix Multiplication

To multiply a matrix by a single number or variable, simply multiply each value within the matrix by that number or variable.

EXAMPLES

59. Simplify: $\begin{bmatrix} 6 & 4 & -8 \\ -3 & 1 & 0 \end{bmatrix} + \begin{bmatrix} 5 & -3 & -2 \\ -3 & 4 & 9 \end{bmatrix}$

60. Solve for x and y: $\begin{bmatrix} x & 6 \\ 4 & y \end{bmatrix} + \begin{bmatrix} 3 & 2 \\ 8 & -1 \end{bmatrix} = \begin{bmatrix} 11 & 8 \\ 12 & 4 \end{bmatrix}$

61. If $\mathbf{A} = \begin{bmatrix} 1 & 3 & 0 \\ 6 & 2 & 4 \end{bmatrix}$ and $\mathbf{B} = \begin{bmatrix} 5 & 3 \\ 2 & 1 \\ 4 & 7 \end{bmatrix}$, what is $\mathbf{AB}$?

62. Simplify: $6x \begin{bmatrix} 2 & -3 \\ 6 & 4 \end{bmatrix}$

Answer Key

1. $\sqrt{5}$ is an irrational number because it cannot be written as a fraction of two integers. It is a decimal that goes on forever without repeating.

2. $-\sqrt{64}$ can be rewritten as the negative whole number −8, so it is an **integer**.

3. Subtract the real and imaginary numbers separately.

    $3 - 1 = 2$

    $5i - (-2i) = 5i + 2i = 7i$

    Solve $(3 + 5i) - (1 - 2i) = 2 + 7i$

4. $(-) \times (+) = (-)$

    $-10 \times 47 = \textbf{−470}$

5. $(-) + (-) = (-)$

    $-65 + -32 = \textbf{−97}$

6. $(-) \times (+) = (-)$

    $-7 \times 4 = -28$, which is **less than −7**

7. $(-) \div (+) = (-)$

    $-16 \div 2.5 = \textbf{−6.4}$

8. First, complete operations within parentheses:

    $-(2)^2 - (11)$

    Second, calculate the value of exponential numbers:

    $-(4) - (11)$

    Finally, do addition and subtraction:

    $-4 - 11 = \textbf{−15}$

9. First, calculate the value of exponential numbers:

    $(25) \div 5 + 4 \times 2$

    Second, calculate division and multiplication from left to right:

    $5 + 8$

    Finally, do addition and subtraction:

    $5 + 8 = \textbf{13}$

10. First, complete operations within parentheses:

    $15 \times (12) - 3^3$

    Second, calculate the value of exponential numbers:

    $15 \times (12) - 27$

    Third, calculate division and multiplication from left to right:

    $180 - 27$

    Finally, do addition and subtraction from left to right:

    $180 - 27 = \textbf{153}$

11. First, complete operations within parentheses:

    $(10) + 23 - 4^2$

    Second, calculate the value of exponential numbers:

    $(10) + 23 - 16$

    Finally, do addition and subtraction from left to right:

    $(10) + 23 - 16$

    $33 - 16 = \textbf{17}$

12. 1 yd. = 3 ft.

    $\frac{15}{3} = \textbf{5 yd.}$

13. 1 gal. = 16 cups

    $\frac{24}{16} = \textbf{1.5 gal.}$

14. 12 in. = 1 ft.

    $\frac{144}{12} = 12$ ft.

    12 ft. × 3 spools = **36 ft. of wire**

15. This problem can be worked in two steps: finding how many inches are covered in 1 minute, and then converting that value to feet. It can also be worked the opposite way, by finding how many feet it travels in 1 second and then converting that to feet traveled per minute. The first method is shown below.

1 min. = 60 sec.

$\frac{6\ in.}{sec.} \times 60\ s = 360\ in.$

1 ft. = 12 in.

$\frac{360\ in.}{12\ in.} =$ **30 ft.**

16. 1 meter = 1000 mm

0.5 meters = **500 mm**

17. 1 kg = 1000 g

$\frac{38\ g}{1000\ g} =$ **0.038 kg**

18. 1 L = 1000 cm^3

10 L = 1000 cm^3 × 10

10 L = **10,000 cm^3**

19. 1 cm = 10 mm

10 cm − 9.6 cm = 0.4 cm lost

0.4 cm = 10 mm × 0.4 = **4 mm were lost**

20.   17.07

   + 2.52

= **19.59**

21.   7.4

   − 6.8

= **0.6 gal.**

22. 25 × 14 = 350

There are 2 digits after the decimal in 0.25 and one digit after the decimal in 1.4. Therefore the product should have 3 digits after the decimal: **0.350 is the correct answer.**

23. Change 0.2 to 2 by moving the decimal one space to the right.

Next, move the decimal one space to the right on the dividend. 0.8 becomes 8.

Now, divide 8 by 2. 8 ÷ 2 = **4**

24. First, change the divisor to a whole number: 0.25 becomes 25.

Next, change the dividend to match the divisor by moving the decimal two spaces to the right, so 40 becomes 4000.

Now divide: 4000 ÷ 25 = **160**

25. 121 and 77 share a common factor of 11. So, if we divide each by 11 we can simplify the fraction:

$\frac{121}{77} = \frac{11}{11} \times \frac{11}{7} = \frac{\mathbf{11}}{\mathbf{7}}$

26. Start by dividing the numerator by the denominator:

37 ÷ 5 = 7 with a remainder of 2.

Now build a mixed number with the whole number and the new numerator:

$\frac{37}{5} = \mathbf{7\frac{2}{5}}$

27. For a fraction division problem, invert the second fraction and then multiply and reduce:

$\frac{7}{8} \div \frac{1}{4} = \frac{7}{8} \times \frac{4}{1} = \frac{28}{8} = \frac{\mathbf{7}}{\mathbf{2}}$

28. This is a fraction multiplication problem, so simply multiply the numerators together and the denominators together and then reduce:

$\frac{1}{12} \times \frac{6}{8} = \frac{6}{96} = \frac{\mathbf{1}}{\mathbf{16}}$

Sometimes it's easier to reduce fractions before multiplying if you can:

$\frac{1}{12} \times \frac{6}{8} = \frac{1}{12} \times \frac{3}{4} = \frac{3}{48} = \frac{\mathbf{1}}{\mathbf{16}}$

29. This is a fraction division problem, so the first step is to convert the mixed number to an improper fraction:

$$1\frac{1}{5} = \frac{5\times 1}{5} + \frac{1}{5} = \frac{6}{5}$$

Now, divide the fractions. Remember to invert the second fraction, and then multiply normally:

$$\frac{2}{5} \div \frac{6}{5} = \frac{2}{5} \times \frac{5}{6} = \frac{10}{30} = \mathbf{\frac{1}{3}}$$

30. This is a fraction multiplication problem: $\frac{1}{4} \times 8\frac{1}{2}$.

First, we need to convert the mixed number into an improper fraction:

$$8\frac{1}{2} = \frac{8\times 2}{2} + \frac{1}{2} = \frac{17}{2}$$

Now, multiply the fractions across the numerators and denominators, and then reduce:

$$\frac{1}{4} \times 8\frac{1}{2} = \frac{1}{4} \times \frac{17}{2} = \mathbf{\frac{17}{8}}\textbf{ cups of sugar}$$

31. First, multiply each fraction by a factor of 1 to get a common denominator.

How do you know which factor of 1 to use? Look at the other fraction and use the number found in that denominator:

$$\frac{2}{3} - \frac{1}{5} = \frac{2}{3}\left(\frac{5}{5}\right) - \frac{1}{5}\left(\frac{3}{3}\right) = \frac{10}{15} - \frac{3}{15}$$

Once the fractions have a common denominator, simply subtract the numerators:

$$\frac{10}{15} - \frac{3}{15} = \mathbf{\frac{7}{15}}$$

32. This is a fraction subtraction problem with a mixed number, so the first step is to convert the mixed number to an improper fraction:

$$2\frac{1}{3} = \frac{2\times 3}{3} + \frac{1}{3} = \frac{7}{3}$$

Next, convert each fraction so they share a common denominator:

$$\frac{7}{3} \times \frac{2}{2} = \frac{14}{6}$$

$$\frac{3}{2} \times \frac{3}{3} = \frac{9}{6}$$

Now, subtract the fractions by subtracting the numerators:

$$\frac{14}{6} - \frac{9}{6} = \mathbf{\frac{5}{6}}$$

33. For this fraction addition problem, we need to find a common denominator. Notice that 2 and 4 are both factors of 16, so 16 can be the common denominator:

$$\frac{1}{2} \times \frac{8}{8} = \frac{8}{16}$$

$$\frac{7}{4} \times \frac{4}{4} = \frac{28}{16}$$

$$\frac{9}{16} + \frac{8}{16} + \frac{28}{16} = \mathbf{\frac{45}{16}}$$

34. To add fractions, make sure that they have a common denominator. Since 3 is a factor of 6, 6 can be the common denominator:

$$\frac{2}{3} \times \frac{2}{2} = \frac{4}{6}$$

Now, add the numerators:

$$\frac{4}{6} + \frac{1}{6} = \mathbf{\frac{5}{6}}\textbf{ of a can}$$

35. The first step here is to simplify the fraction:

$$\frac{8}{18} = \frac{4}{9}$$

Now it's clear that the fraction is a multiple of $\frac{1}{9}$, so you can easily find the decimal using a value you already know:

$$\frac{4}{9} = \frac{1}{9} \times 4 = 0.\overline{11} \times 4 = \mathbf{0.\overline{44}}$$

36. None of the tricks above will work for this fraction, so you need to do long division:

```
        0.1875
   16 ) 3.0000
      - 1.6000
        1.40
      - 1.28
        0.120
      - 0.112
        0.0080
      - 0.0080
        0.0000
```

The decimal will go in front of the answer, so now you know that $\frac{3}{16}$ = **0.1875.**

37. The last number in the decimal is in the hundredths place, so we can easily set up a fraction:

$$0.45 = \frac{45}{100}$$

The next step is simply to reduce the fraction down to the lowest common denominator. Here, both 45 and 100 are divisible by 5. 45 divided by 5 is 9, and 100 divided by 5 is 20. Therefore, you're left with:

$$\frac{45}{100} = \mathbf{\frac{9}{20}}$$

38. We know that there are 5 Democrats for every 4 Republicans in the room, which means for every 9 people, 4 are Republicans.

$$5 + 4 = 9$$

Fraction of Democrats: $\frac{5}{9}$
Fraction of Republicans: $\frac{4}{9}$
If $\frac{4}{9}$ of the 90 voters are Republicans, then:
$$\frac{4}{9} \times 90 = \mathbf{40 \ voters \ are}$$
Republicans

39. To solve this ratio problem, we can simply multiply both sides of the ratio by the desired value to find the number of students that correspond to having 38 teachers:

$$\frac{15 \ students}{1 \ teacher} \times 38 \ teachers = 570$$
students

The school has **570 students.**

40. Start by setting up the proportion:

$$\frac{120 \ mi}{3 \ hrs} = \frac{180 mi}{x \ hr}$$

Note that it doesn't matter which value is placed in the numerator or denominator, as long as it is the same on both sides. Now, solve for the missing quantity through cross-multiplication:

$$120 \ mi \times x \ hr = 3 \ hrs \times 180 \ mi$$

Now solve the equation:

$$x \ hours = \frac{3 \ hrs \times 180 \ mi}{120 \ mi}$$

$$x = \mathbf{4.5 \ hrs}$$

41. Set up the equation:

$$\frac{1 \ acre}{500 \ gal} = \frac{x \ acres}{2600 \ gal}$$

Then solve for x:

$$x \ acres = \frac{1 \ acre \times 2600 \ gal}{500 \ gal}$$

$$x = \frac{26}{5} \ acres \ or \ \mathbf{5.2 \ acres}$$

42. This problem presents two equivalent ratios that can be set up in a fraction equation:

$$\frac{35}{5} = \frac{49}{x}$$

You can then cross-multiply to solve for x:

$$35x = 49 \times 5$$

$$\mathbf{x = 7}$$

43. Set up the appropriate equation and solve. Don't forget to change 15% to a decimal value:

$$whole = \frac{part}{percent} = \frac{45}{0.15} = \mathbf{300}$$

44. Set up the appropriate equation and solve:

$$whole = \frac{part}{percent} = \frac{15 + 30 + 20}{.30} =$$
$217.00

45. Set up the equation and solve:

$$percent = \frac{part}{whole} = \frac{39}{65} = \mathbf{0.6 \ or \ 60\%}$$

46. You can use the information in the question to figure out what percentage of subscriptions were sold by Max and Greta:

$$percent = \frac{part}{whole} = \frac{51 + 45}{240} = \frac{96}{240} =$$
0.4 or 40%

However, the question asks how many subscriptions weren't sold by Max or Greta. If they sold 40%, then the other salespeople sold 100% − 40% = 60%.

47. Set up the equation and solve. Remember to convert 75% to a decimal value:

part = whole × percent = 45 × 0.75 = 33.75, so **he needs to answer at least 34 questions correctly.**

48. Set up the appropriate equation and solve:

amount of change = original amount × percent change →

25 × 0.4 = 10

If the amount of change is 10, that means the store adds a markup of $10, so the game costs:

$25 + $10 = **$35**

49. First, calculate the amount of change:

75 − 40 = 35

Now you can set up the equation and solve. (Note that markup rate is another way of saying percent change):

$$\text{percent change} = \frac{\text{amount of change}}{\text{original amount}}$$

$$\rightarrow \quad \frac{35}{40} = 0.875 = \textbf{87.5\%}$$

50. You're solving for the original price, but it's going to be tricky because you don't know the amount of change; you only know the new price. To solve, you need to create an expression for the amount of change:

If original amount = x

Then amount of change = 63 − x

Now you can plug these values into your equation:

$$\text{original amount} = \frac{\text{amount of change}}{\text{percent change}}$$

$$x = \frac{63 - x}{0.4}$$

The last step is to solve for x:

$$0.4x = 63 - x$$

$1.4x = 63$

$x = 45 \rightarrow$ **The store paid $45 for the shoes.**

51. You've been asked to find the sale price, which means you need to solve for the amount of change first:

amount of change = original amount × percent change =

55 × 0.25 = 13.75

Using this amount, you can find the new price. Because it's on sale, we know the item will cost less than the original price:

55 − 13.75 = 41.25

The sale price is **$41.25**.

52. This problem is tricky because you need to figure out what each number in the problem stands for. 24% is obviously the percent change, but what about the measurements in feet? If you multiply these values you get the area of the garden (for more on area see *Area and Perimeter*):

18 ft. × 51 ft. = 918 ft.^{2}

This 918 ft.^{2} is the amount of change—it's how much area the yard lost to create the garden. Now you can set up an equation:

$$\text{original amount} = \frac{\text{amount of change}}{\text{percent change}}$$

$$= \frac{918}{.24} = 3825$$

If the original lawn was 3825 ft.^{2} and the garden is 918 ft.^{2}, then the remaining area is:

3825 − 918 = 2907

The remaining lawn covers 2907 ft.^{2}

53. These numbers are in different formats—one is a mixed fraction and the other is just a fraction. So, the first step is to convert the mixed fraction to a fraction:

$$4\frac{3}{4} = \frac{4 \times 4}{4} + \frac{3}{4} = \frac{19}{4}$$

Once the mixed number is converted, it is easier to see that

$\frac{19}{4}$ **is greater than** $\frac{18}{4}$.

54. These numbers are already in the same format, so the decimal values just need to be compared. Remember that zeros can be added after the decimal without changing the value, so the three numbers can be rewritten as:

104.56

104.50

104.60

From this list, it is clear that **104.60 is the greatest** because 0.60 is larger than 0.50 and 0.56.

55. The first step is to convert the numbers into the same format—65% is the same as $\frac{65}{100}$.

Next, the fractions need to be converted to have the same denominator because it is difficult to compare fractions with different denominators. Using a factor of $\frac{5}{5}$ on the second fraction will give common denominators:

$\frac{13}{20} \times \frac{5}{5} = \frac{65}{100}$. Now it is easy to see that **the numbers are equivalent.**

56. When multiplying exponents in which the base number is the same, simply add the powers:

$$2^4 \times 2^2 = 2^{(4+2)} = 2^6$$

$$2^6 = 2 \times 2 \times 2 \times 2 \times 2 \times 2 = \mathbf{64}$$

57. When an exponent is raised to a power, multiply the powers:

$$(3^4)^{-1} = 3^{-4}$$

When the exponent is a negative number, rewrite as the reciprocal of the positive exponent:

$$3^{-4} = \frac{1}{3^4}$$

$$\frac{1}{3^4} = \frac{1}{3 \times 3 \times 3 \times 3} = \frac{1}{81}$$

58. When the power is a fraction, rewrite as a radical:

$$\left(\frac{9}{4}\right)^{\frac{1}{2}} = \sqrt{\frac{9}{4}}$$

Next, distribute the radical to the numerator and denominator:

$$\sqrt{\frac{9}{4}} = \frac{\sqrt{9}}{\sqrt{4}} = \frac{3}{2}$$

59. Add each corresponding number:

$$\begin{bmatrix} 6+5 & 4+(-3) & (-8)+(-2) \\ (-3)+(-3) & 1+4 & 0+9 \end{bmatrix} = \begin{bmatrix} \mathbf{11} & \mathbf{1} & \mathbf{-10} \\ \mathbf{-6} & \mathbf{5} & \mathbf{9} \end{bmatrix}$$

60. Add each corresponding number to create 2 equations:

$$\begin{bmatrix} x+3 & 6+2 \\ 4+8 & y+(-1) \end{bmatrix} = \begin{bmatrix} 11 & 8 \\ 12 & 4 \end{bmatrix}$$

$x + 3 = 11$

$y - 1 = 4$

Now, solve each equation:

$\mathbf{x = 8, y = 5}$

61. First, check to see that they can be multiplied: **A** has 3 columns and **B** has 3 rows, so they can. The resulting matrix will be 2 × 2. Now multiply the numbers in the first row of **A** by the numbers in the first column of **B** and add the results:

$$\begin{bmatrix} 1 & 3 & 0 \\ 6 & 2 & 4 \end{bmatrix} \times \begin{bmatrix} 5 & 3 \\ 2 & 1 \\ 4 & 7 \end{bmatrix} = \begin{bmatrix} (1 \times 5) + (3 \times 2) + (0 \times 4) & \square \\ \square & \square \end{bmatrix} = \begin{bmatrix} \mathbf{11} & \square \\ \square & \square \end{bmatrix}$$

Now, multiply and add to find the 3 missing values:

$$\begin{bmatrix} 1 & 3 & 0 \\ 6 & 2 & 4 \end{bmatrix} \times \begin{bmatrix} 5 & 3 \\ 2 & 1 \\ 4 & 7 \end{bmatrix} =$$

$$\begin{bmatrix} (1 \times 5) + (3 \times 2) + (0 \times 4) & (1 \times 3) + (3 \times 1) + (0 \times 7) \\ (6 \times 5) + (2 \times 2) + (4 \times 4) & (6 \times 3) + (2 \times 1) + (4 \times 7) \end{bmatrix} = \begin{bmatrix} \mathbf{11} & \mathbf{6} \\ \mathbf{50} & \mathbf{48} \end{bmatrix}$$

62. Multiply each value inside the matrix by $6x$.

$$6x \begin{bmatrix} 2 & -3 \\ 6 & 4 \end{bmatrix} = \begin{bmatrix} 6x \times 2 & 6x \times (-3) \\ 6x \times 6 & 6x \times 4 \end{bmatrix} = \begin{bmatrix} \mathbf{12x} & \mathbf{-18x} \\ \mathbf{36x} & \mathbf{24x} \end{bmatrix}$$

CHAPTER FOUR
Algebra

Algebraic Expressions

Algebraic expressions and equations include **VARIABLES**, or letters standing in for numbers. These expressions and equations are made up of **TERMS**, which are groups of numbers and variables (e.g., $2xy$). An **EXPRESSION** is simply a set of terms (e.g., $\frac{2x}{3yz} + 2$). When those terms are joined only by addition or subtraction, the expression is called a polynomial (e.g., $2x + 3yz$). When working with expressions, you'll need to use many different mathematical properties and operations, including addition/subtraction, multiplication/division, exponents, roots, distribution, and the order of operations.

EVALUATING ALGEBRAIC EXPRESSIONS

To evaluate an algebraic expression, simply plug the given value(s) in for the appropriate variable(s) in the expression.

EXAMPLE

1. Evaluate $2x + 6y - 3z$ if $x = 2$, $y = 4$, and $z = -3$.

ADDING and SUBTRACTING EXPRESSIONS

Only **LIKE TERMS**, which have the exact same variable(s), can be added or subtracted. **CONSTANTS** are numbers without variables attached, and those can be added and subtracted together as well. When simplifying an expression, like terms should be added or subtracted so that no individual group of variables occurs in more than one term. For example, the expression $5x + 6xy$ is in its simplest form, while $5x + 6xy - 11xy$ is not because the term xy appears more than once.

2. Simplify the expression: $5xy + 7y + 2yz + 11xy - 5yz$

MULTIPLYING and DIVIDING EXPRESSIONS

To multiply a single term by another, simply multiply the coefficients and then multiply the variables. Remember that when multiplying variables with exponents, those exponents are added together. For example: $(x^5y)(x^3y^4) = x^8y^5$.

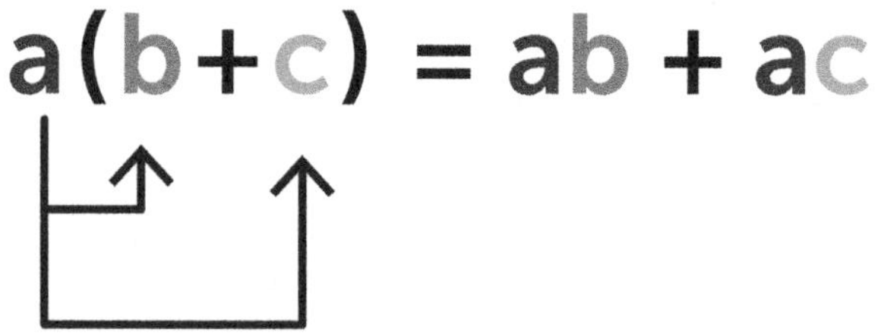

$$a(b+c) = ab + ac$$

Figure 4.1. Distribution

When multiplying a term by a set of terms inside parentheses, you need to distribute to each term inside the parentheses as shown in Figure 4.1.

When variables occur in both the numerator and denominator of a fraction, they cancel each other out. So, a fraction with variables in its simplest form will not have the same variable on the top and bottom.

EXAMPLES

3. Simplify the expression: $(3x^4 y^2z)(2y^4z^5)$

4. Simplify the expression: $(2y^2)(y^3 + 2xy^2z + 4z)$

5. Simplify the expression: $(5x + 2)(3x + 3)$

6. Simplify the expression: $\frac{2x^4y^3z}{8x^2z^2}$

FACTORING EXPRESSIONS

Factoring is splitting one expression into the multiplication of two expressions. It requires finding the highest common factor and dividing terms by that number. For example, in the expression $15x + 10$, the highest common factor is 5 because both terms are divisible by 5: $\frac{15x}{5} = 3x$ and $\frac{10}{5} = 2$. When you factor the expression you get $5(3x + 2)$.

Sometimes it is difficult to find the highest common factor. In these cases, consider whether the expression fits a polynomial identity. A polynomial is an expression with more than one term. If you can recognize the common polynomials listed below, you can easily factor the expression.

► $a^2 - b^2 = (a + b)(a - b)$

► $a^2 + 2ab + b^2 = (a + b)(a + b) = (a + b)^2$

► $a^2 - 2ab + b^2 = (a - b)(a - b) = (a - b)^2$

► $a^3 + b^3 = (a + b)(a^2 - ab + b^2)$

► $a^3 - b^3 = (a - b)(a^2 + ab + b^2)$

7. Factor the expression: $27x^2 - 9x$

8. Factor the expression: $25x^2 - 16$

9. Factor the expression: $100x^2 + 60x + 9$

Linear Equations

An **EQUATION** is a statement saying that two expressions are equal to each other. They always include an equal sign (e.g., $3x + 2xy = 17$). A **LINEAR EQUATION** has only two variables; on a graph, linear equations form a straight line.

SOLVING LINEAR EQUATIONS

To solve an equation, you need to manipulate the terms on each side to isolate the variable, meaning if you want to find x, you have to get the x alone on one side of the equal sign. To do this, you'll need to use many of the tools discussed above: you might need to distribute, divide, add, or subtract like terms, or find common denominators.

Think of each side of the equation as the two sides of a see-saw. As long as the two people on each end weigh the same amount (no matter what it is) the see-saw will be balanced: if you have a 120 pound person on each end, the see-saw is balanced. Giving each of them a 10 pound rock to hold changes the weight on each end, but the see-saw itself stays balanced. Equations work the same way: you can add, subtract, multiply, or divide whatever you want as long as you do the same thing to both sides.

DID YOU KNOW?
If you're stumped, try plugging the answer choices back into the original problem to see which one works.

Most equations you'll see on the SAT can be solved using the same basic steps:

1. distribute to get rid of parentheses
2. use LCD to get rid of fractions
3. add/subtract like terms on either side
4. add/subtract so that constants appear on only one side of the equation
5. multiply/divide to isolate the variable

EXAMPLES

10. Solve for x: $25x + 12 = 62$

11. Solve the following equation for x: $2x - 4(2x + 3) = 24$

12. Solve the following equation for x: $\frac{x}{3} + \frac{1}{2} = \frac{x}{6} - \frac{5}{12}$

13. Find the value of x: $2(x + y) - 7x = 14x + 3$

GRAPHING LINEAR EQUATIONS

Linear equations can be plotted as straight lines on a coordinate plane. The **x-AXIS** is always the horizontal axis and the **y-AXIS** is always the vertical axis. The x-axis is positive to the right of the y-axis and negative to the left. The y-axis is positive above the x-axis and negative below. To describe the location of any point on the graph, write the coordinates in the form (x, y). The origin, the point where the x- and y-axes cross, is $(0, 0)$.

The **y-INTERCEPT** is the y coordinate where the line crosses the y-axis. The **SLOPE** is a measure of how steep the line is. Slope is calculated by dividing the change along the y-axis by the change along the x-axis between any two points on the line.

Linear equations are easiest to graph when they are written in **POINT-SLOPE FORM**: $y = mx + b$. The constant m represents slope and the constant b represents the y-intercept. If you know two points along the line (x_1, y_1) and (x_2, y_2), you can calculate slope using the following equation: $m = \frac{y_2 - y_1}{x_2 - x_1}$. If you know the slope and one other point along the line, you can calculate the y-intercept by plugging the number 0 in for x_2 and solving for y_2.

When graphing a linear equation, first plot the y-intercept. Next, plug in values for x to solve for y and plot additional points. Connect the points with a straight line.

EXAMPLES

14. Find the slope of the line: $\frac{3y}{2} + 3 = x$

15. Plot the linear equation: $2y - 4x = 6$

SYSTEMS of EQUATIONS

A system of equations is a group of related questions sharing the same variable. The problems you see on the SAT will most likely involve two equations that each have two variables, although you may also solve sets of equations with any number of variables as long as there are a corresponding number of equations (e.g., to solve a system with four variables, you need four equations).

DID YOU KNOW?
The math section will always include a set of questions that require you to understand and manipulate a real-life equation (usually related to physics).

There are two main methods used to solve systems of equations. In **SUBSTITUTION**, solve one equation for a single variable, then substitute the solution for that variable into the second equation to solve for the other variable. Or, you can use **ELIMINATION** by adding equations together to cancel variables and solve for one of them.

16. Solve the following system of equations: $3y - 4 + x = 0$ and $5x + 6y = 11$

17. Solve the system: $2x + 4y = 8$ and $4x + 2y = 10$

BUILDING EQUATIONS

Word problems describe a situation or a problem without explicitly providing an equation to solve. It is up to you to build an algebraic equation to solve the problem. You must translate the words into mathematical operations. Represent the quantity you do not know with a variable. If there is more than one unknown, you will likely have to write more than one equation, then solve the system of equations by substituting expressions. Make sure you keep your variables straight!

EXAMPLES

18. David, Jesse, and Mark shoveled snow during their snow day and made a total of $100. They agreed to split it based on how much each person worked. David will take $10 more than Jesse, who will take $15 more than Mark. How much money will David get?

19. The sum of three consecutive numbers is 54. What is the middle number?

20. There are 42 people on the varsity football team. This is 8 more than half the number of people on the swim team. There are 6 fewer boys on the swim team than girls. How many girls are on the swim team?

Linear Inequalities

INEQUALITIES look like equations, except that instead of having an equal sign, they have one of the following symbols:

> greater than: the expression left of the symbol is larger than the expression on the right

< less than: the expression left of the symbol is smaller than the expression on the right

≥ greater than or equal to: the expression left of the symbol is larger than or equal to the expression on the right

≤ less than or equal to: the expression left of the symbol is less than or equal to the expression on the right

SOLVING LINEAR INEQUALITIES

Inequalities are solved like linear and algebraic equations. The only difference is that the symbol must be reversed when both sides of the equation are multiplied by a negative number.

EXAMPLE

21. Solve for x: $-7x + 2 < 6 - 5x$

GRAPHING LINEAR INEQUALITIES

Graphing a linear inequality is just like graphing a linear equation, except that you shade the area on one side of the line. To graph a linear inequality, first rearrange the inequality expression into $y = mx + b$ form. Then treat the inequality symbol like an equal sign and plot the line. If the inequality symbol is < or >, make a broken line; for ≤ or ≥, make a solid line. Finally, shade the correct side of the graph:

> For $y < mx + b$ or $y \leq mx + b$, shade **below** the line.
>
> For $y > mx + b$ or $y \geq mx + b$, shade **above** the line.

EXAMPLE

22. Plot the inequality: $-3 \geq 4 - y$

Quadratic Equations

A quadratic equation is any equation in the form $ax^2 + bx + c = 0$. In quadratic equations, x is the variable and a, b, and c are all known numbers. a cannot be 0.

SOLVING QUADRATIC EQUATIONS

There is more than one way to solve a quadratic equation. One way is by **FACTORING**. By rearranging the expression $ax^2 + bx + c$ into one factor multiplied by another factor, you can easily solve for the **ROOTS**, the values of x for which the quadratic expression equals 0. Another way to solve a quadratic equation is by using the **QUADRATIC FORMULA**:

$$x = \frac{-b \pm \sqrt{b^2 - 4ac}}{2a}$$

The expression $b^2 - 4ac$ is called the **DISCRIMINANT**; when it is positive you will get two real numbers for x, when it is negative you will get one real number and one imaginary number for x, and when it is zero you will get one real number for x.

23. Factor the quadratic equation $-2x^2 = 14x$ and find the roots.

24. Use the quadratic formula to solve for x: $3x^2 = 7x - 2$.

GRAPHING QUADRATIC EQUATIONS

Graphing a quadratic equation forms a **PARABOLA**. A parabola is a symmetrical, horseshoe-shaped curve; a vertical axis passes through its vertex. Each term in the equation $ax^2 + bx + c = 0$ affects the shape of the parabola. A bigger value for a makes the curve narrower, while a smaller value makes the curve wider. A negative value for a flips the parabola upside down. The **AXIS OF SYMMETRY** is the vertical line $x = \frac{-b}{2a}$. To find the y-coordinate for the **VERTEX** (the highest or lowest point on the parabola), plug this value for x into the expression $ax^2 + bx + c$. The easiest way to graph a quadratic equation is to find the axis of symmetry, solve for the vertex, and then create a table of points by plugging in other numbers for x and solving for y. Plot these points and trace the parabola.

EXAMPLE

25. Graph the equation: $x^2 + 4x + 1 = 0$

Functions

FUNCTIONS describe how an input relates to an output. Linear equations, sine, and cosine are examples of functions. In a function, there must be one and only one output for each input. $\sqrt{x}$ is not a function because there are two outputs for any one input: $\sqrt{4} = 2, -2$.

DESCRIBING FUNCTIONS

Functions are often written in $f(x)$ form: $f(x) = x^2$ means that for input x the output is x^2. In relating functions to linear equations, you can think of $f(x)$ as equivalent to y. The **DOMAIN** of a function is all the possible inputs of that function. The **RANGE** of a function includes the outputs of the inputs. For example, for the function $f(x) = x^2$, if the domain includes all positive and negative integers the range will include 0 and only positive integers. When you graph a function, the domain is plotted on the x-axis and the range is plotted on the y-axis.

EXAMPLES

26. Given $f(x) = 2x - 10$, find $f(9)$.

27. Given $f(x) = \frac{4}{x}$ with a domain of all positive integers except zero, and $g(x) = \frac{4}{x}$ with a domain of all positive and negative integers except zero, which function has a range that includes the number -2?

EXPONENTIAL FUNCTIONS

An **EXPONENTIAL FUNCTION** is in the form $f(x) = a^x$, where $a > 0$. When $a > 1$, $f(x)$ approaches infinity as x increases and zero as x decreases. When $0 < a < 1$, $f(x)$ approaches zero as x increases and infinity as x increases. When $a = 1$, $f(x) = 1$. The graph of an exponential function where $a \neq 1$ will have a horizontal asymptote along the x-axis; the graph will never cross below the x-axis. The graph of an exponential function where $a = 1$ will be a horizontal line at $y = 1$. All graphs of exponential functions include the points $(0, 1)$ and $(1, a)$.

EXAMPLES

28. Graph the function: $f(x) = 3^x$.

29. Given $f(x) = 2^x$, solve for x when $f(x) = 64$.

LOGARITHMIC FUNCTIONS

A **LOGARITHMIC FUNCTION** is the inverse of an exponential function. Remember the definition of a log: if $\log_a x = b$, then $a^b = x$. Logarithmic functions are written in the form $f(x) = \log_a x$, where a is any number greater than 0, except for 1. If a is not shown, it is assumed that $a = 10$. The function $\ln x$ is called a **NATURAL LOG**, equal to $\log_e x$. When $0 < a < 1$, $f(x)$ approaches infinity as x approaches zero and negative infinity as x increases. When $a > 1$, $f(x)$ approaches negative infinity as x approaches zero and infinity as x increases. In either case, the graph of a logarithmic function has a vertical asymptote along the y-axis; the graph will never cross to the left of the y-axis. All graphs of logarithmic functions include the points $(1, 0)$ and $(a, 1)$.

EXAMPLES

30. Graph the function $f(x) = \log_4 x$.

31. Given $f(x) = \log_{\frac{1}{3}} x$, solve for $f(81)$.

ARITHMETIC and GEOMETRIC SEQUENCES

SEQUENCES are patterns of numbers. In most questions about sequences you must determine the pattern. In an **ARITHMETIC SEQUENCE**, add or subtract the same number between terms. In a **GEOMETRIC SEQUENCE**, multiply or divide by the same number between terms. For example, 2, 6, 10, 14, 18 and 11, 4, –3, –10, –17 are arithmetic sequences because you add 4 to each term in the first example and you subtract 7 from each term in the second example. The sequence 5, 15, 45, 135 is a geometric sequence because you multiply each term by 3. In arithmetic sequences, the number by which you add or subtract is called the **COMMON DIFFERENCE**. In geometric sequences, the number by which you multiply or divide is called the **COMMON RATIO**.

In an arithmetic sequence, the nth term (a_n) can be found by calculating $a_n = a_1 + (n - 1)d$, where d is the common difference and a_1 is the first term in the sequence. In a geometric sequence, $a_n = a_1(r^n)$, where r is the common ratio.

EXAMPLES

32. Find the common difference and the next term of the following sequence: 5, –1, –7, –13

33. Find the twelfth term of the following sequence: 2, 6, 18, 54

34. The fourth term of a sequence is 9. The common difference is 11. What is the tenth term?

Absolute Value

The **ABSOLUTE VALUE** of a number (represented by the symbol $||$) is its distance from zero, not its value. For example, $|3| = 3$, and $|-3| = 3$ because both 3 and –3 are three units from zero. The absolute value of a number is always positive.

Equations with absolute values will have two answers, so you need to set up two equations. The first is simply the equation with the absolute value symbol removed. For the second equation, isolate the absolute value on one side of the equation and multiply the other side of the equation by –1.

EXAMPLES

35. Solve for x: $|2x - 3| = x + 1$

36. Solve for y: $2|y + 4| = 10$

Solving Word Problems

Any of the math concepts discussed here can be turned into a word problem, and you'll likely see word problems in various formats throughout the test. (In fact, you may have noticed that several examples in the ratio and proportion sections were word problems.)

Be sure to read the entire problem before beginning to solve it: a common mistake is to provide an answer to a question that wasn't actually asked. Also, remember that not all of the information provided in a problem is necessarily needed to solve it.

When working multiple-choice word problems like those on the SAT, it's important to check your work. Many of the incorrect answer choices will be answers that result from common mistakes. So even if a solution you calculated is listed as an answer choice, that doesn't necessarily mean you've done the problem correctly—you have to check your own answer to be sure.

Some general steps for word-problem solving are:

1. Read the entire problem and determine what the question is asking.
2. List all of the given data and define the variables.
3. Determine the formula(s) needed or set up equations from the information in the problem.
4. Solve.
5. Check your answer. (Is the amount too large or small? Is the answer in the correct unit of measure?)

Word problems generally contain **KEY WORDS** that can help you determine what math processes may be required in order to solve them.

▶ **Addition**: *added, combined, increased by, in all, total, perimeter, sum*, and *more than*

▶ **Subtraction**: *how much more, less than, fewer than, exceeds, difference*, and *decreased*

▶ **Multiplication**: *of, times, area*, and *product*

▶ **Division**: *distribute, share, average, per, out of, percent*, and *quotient*

▶ **Equals**: *is, was, are, amounts to*, and *were*

BASIC WORD PROBLEMS

A word problem in algebra is just an equation or a set of equations described using words. Your task when solving these problems is to turn the *story* of the problem into mathematical equations. Converting units can often help you avoid operations with fractions when dealing with time.

EXAMPLES

37. A store owner bought a case of 48 backpacks for $476.00. He sold 17 of the backpacks in his store for $18 each, and the rest were sold to a school for $15 each. What was the store owner's profit?

38. Thirty students in Mr. Joyce's room are working on projects over 2 days. The first day, he gave them $\frac{3}{5}$ hour to work. On the second day, he gave them $\frac{1}{2}$ as much time as the first day. How much time did each student have to work on the project?

DISTANCE WORD PROBLEMS

Distance word problems involve something traveling at a constant or average speed. Whenever you read a problem that involves *how fast*, *how far*, or *for how long*, you should think of the distance equation, where *d* stands for distance, *r* for rate (speed), and *t* for time.

These problems can be solved by setting up a grid with *d*, *r*, and *t* along the top and each moving object on the left. When setting up the grid, make sure the units are consistent. For example, if the distance is in meters and the time is in seconds, the rate should be meters per second.

EXAMPLES

39. Will drove from his home to the airport at an average speed of 30 mph. He then boarded a helicopter and flew to the hospital at an average speed of 60 mph. The entire distance was 150 miles, and the trip took 3 hours. Find the distance from the airport to the hospital.

40. Two riders on horseback start at the same time from opposite ends of a field that is 45 miles long. One horse is moving at 14 mph and the second horse is moving at 16 mph. How long after they begin will they meet?

WORK PROBLEMS

Work problems involve situations where several people or machines are doing work at different rates. Your task is usually to figure out how long it will take these people or machines to complete a task while working together. The trick to doing work problems is to figure out how much of the project each person or machine completes in the same unit of time. For example, you might calculate how much of a wall a person can paint in 1 hour, or how many boxes an assembly line can pack in 1 minute.

DID YOU KNOW?

The SAT will give you most formulas you need to work problems, but they won't give you the formulas for percent change or work problems.

The next step is to set up an equation to solve for the total time. This equation is usually similar to the equation for distance, but here *work = rate × time*.

EXAMPLES

41. Bridget can clean an entire house in 12 hours while her brother Tom takes 8 hours. How long would it take for Bridget and Tom to clean 2 houses together?

42. Farmer Dan needs to water his cornfield. One hose can water a field 1.25 times faster than a second hose. When both hoses are running, they water the field together in 5 hours. How long would it take to water the field if only the slower hose is used?

43. Ben takes 2 hours to pick 500 apples, and Frank takes 3 hours to pick 450 apples. How long will they take, working together, to pick 1000 apples?

Answer Key

1. Plug in each number for the correct variable and simplify:

   $2x + 6y - 3z = 2(2) + 6(4) - 3(-3) =$
   $4 + 24 + 9 = $ **37**

2. Start by grouping together like terms:

   $(5xy + 11xy) + (2yz - 5yz) + 7y$

   Now you can add together each set of like terms:

   $16xy + 7y - 3yz$

3. Multiply the coefficients and variables together:

   $3 \times 2 = 6$

   $y^2 \times y^4 = y^6$

   $z \times z^5 = z^6$

   Now put all the terms back together:

   $6x^4y^6z^6$

4. Multiply each term inside the parentheses by the term $2y^2$:

   $(2y^2)(y^3 + 2xy^2z + 4z) =$

   $(2y^2 \times y^3) + (2y^2 \times 2xy^2z) +$
   $(2y^2 \times 4z) =$

   $2y^5 + 4xy^4z + 8y^2z$

5. Use the acronym FOIL—first, outer, inner, last—to multiply the terms:

   first: $5x \times 3x = 15x^2$

   outer: $5x \times 3 = 15x$

   inner: $2 \times 3x = 6x$

   last: $2 \times 3 = 6$

   Now combine like terms:

   $15x^2 + 21x + 6$

6. Simplify by looking at each variable and checking for those that appear in the numerator and denominator:

$\frac{2}{8} = \frac{1}{4}$

$\frac{x^4}{x^2} = \frac{x^2}{1}$

$\frac{z}{z^2} = \frac{1}{z}$

$\frac{2x^4y^3z}{8x^2z^2} = \frac{x^2y^3}{4z}$

7. First, find the highest common factor. Both terms are divisible by 9:

   $\frac{27x^2}{9} = 3x^2$ and $\frac{9x}{9} = x$.

   Now the expression is $9(3x^2 - x)$. But wait, you're not done! Both terms can be divided by x:

   $\frac{3x^2}{x} = 3x$ and $\frac{x}{x} = 1$.

   The final factored expression is **$9x(3x - 1)$**.

8. Since there is no obvious factor by which you can divide terms, you should consider whether this expression fits one of your polynomial identities. This expression is a difference of squares: $a^2 - b^2$, where $a^2 = 25x^2$ and $b^2 = 16$.

   Recall that $a^2 - b^2 = (a + b)(a - b)$. Now solve for a and b:

   $a = \sqrt{25x^2} = 5x$

   $b = \sqrt{16} = 4$

   $(a + b)(a - b) = $ **$(5x + 4)(5x - 4)$**

   You can check your work by using the FOIL acronym to expand your answer back to the original expression:

   first: $5x \times 5x = 25x^2$

   outer: $5x \times -4 = -20x$

   inner: $4 \times 5x = 20x$

   last: $4 \times {-4} = -16$

   $25x^2 - 20x + 20x - 16 = 25x^2 - 16$

9. This is another polynomial identity, $a^2 + 2ab + b^2$. (The more you practice these problems, the faster you will recognize polynomial identities.)

$a^2 = 100x^2$, $2ab = 60x$, and $b^2 = 9$

Recall that $a^2 + 2ab + b^2 = (a + b)^2$. Now solve for a and b:

$a = \sqrt{100x^2} = 10x$

$b = \sqrt{9} = 3$

(Double check your work by confirming that $2ab = 2 \times 10x \times 3 = 60x$)

$(a + b)^2 = \mathbf{(10x + 3)^2}$

10. This equation has no parentheses, fractions, or like terms on the same side, so you can start by subtracting 12 from both sides of the equation:

$25x + 12 = 62$

$(25x + 12) - 12 = 62 - 12$

$25x = 50$

Now, divide by 25 to isolate the variable:

$\frac{25x}{25} = \frac{50}{25}$

$\mathbf{x = 2}$

11. Start by distributing to get rid of the parentheses (don't forget to distribute the negative):

$2x - 4(2x + 3) = 24 \rightarrow$

$2x - 8x - 12 = 24$

There are no fractions, so now you can join like terms:

$2x - 8x - 12 = 24 \rightarrow -6x - 12 = 24$

Now add 12 to both sides and divide by −6.

$-6x - 12 = 24 \rightarrow$

$(-6x - 12) + 12 = 24 + 12 \rightarrow$

$-6x = 36 \rightarrow \frac{-6x}{-6} = \frac{36}{-6}$

$\mathbf{x = -6}$

12. Start by multiplying by the least common denominator to get rid of the fractions:

$\frac{x}{3} + \frac{1}{2} = \frac{x}{6} - \frac{5}{12} \rightarrow$

$12\left(\frac{x}{3} + \frac{1}{2}\right) = 12\left(\frac{x}{6} - \frac{5}{12}\right) \rightarrow$

$4x + 6 = 2x - 5$

Now you can isolate the x:

$(4x + 6) - 6 = (2x - 5) - 6 \rightarrow$

$4x = 2x - 11 \rightarrow$

$(4x) - 2x = (2x - 11) - 2x \rightarrow$

$2x = -11$

$\mathbf{x = -\frac{11}{2}}$

13. This equation looks more difficult because it has 2 variables, but you can use the same steps to solve for x. First, distribute to get rid of the parentheses and combine like terms:

$2(x + y) - 7x = 14x + 3 \rightarrow$

$2x + 2y - 7x = 14x + 3 \rightarrow$

$-5x + 2y = 14x + 3$

Now you can move the x terms to one side and everything else to the other, and then divide to isolate x:

$-5x + 2y = 14x + 3 \rightarrow$

$-19x = -2y + 3 \rightarrow$

$\mathbf{x = \frac{2y - 3}{19}}$

14. Slope is easiest to find when the equation is in point-slope form: $(y = mx + b)$. Rearrange the equation to isolate y:

$\frac{3y}{2} + 3 = x$

$3y + 6 = 2x$

$y + 2 = \frac{2x}{3}$

$y = \frac{2x}{3} - 2$

Finally, identify the term m to find the slope of the line:

$\mathbf{m = \frac{2}{3}}$

15. First, rearrange the linear equation to point-slope form

$(y = mx + b)$:

$2y - 4x = 6$

$y = 2x + 3$

Next, identify the y-intercept (b) and the slope (m):

$b = 3$, $m = 2$

Now, plot the y-intercept $(0,b) = (0,3)$:

Next, plug in values for x and solve for y:

$y = 2(1) + 3 = 5 \rightarrow (1,5)$

$y = 2(-1) + 3 = 1 \rightarrow (-1,1)$

Plot these points on the graph, and connect the points with a straight line:

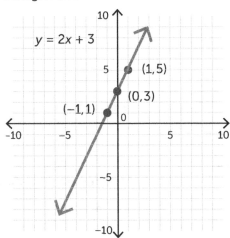

16. To solve this system using substitution, first solve one equation for a single variable:

$3y - 4 + x = 0$

$3y + x = 4$

$x = 4 - 3y$

Next, substitute the expression to the right of the equal sign for x in the second equation:

$5x + 6y = 11$

$5(4 - 3y) + 6y = 11$

$20 - 15y + 6y = 11$

$20 - 9y = 11$

$-9y = -9$

$y = 1$

Finally, plug the value for y back into the first equation to find the value of x:

$3y - 4 + x = 0$

$3(1) - 4 + x = 0$

$-1 + x = 0$

$x = 1$

The solution is **$x = 1$ and $y = 1$**, or the point **(1,1)**.

17. To solve this system using elimination, start by manipulating one equation so that a variable (in this case x) will cancel when the equations are added together:

$2x + 4y = 8$

$-2(2x + 4y = 8)$

$-4x - 8y = -16$

Now you can add the two equations together, and the x variable will drop out:

$-4x - 8y = -16$

$\underline{4x + 2y = 10}$

$-6y = -6$

$y = 1$

Lastly, plug the y value into one of the equations to find the value of x:

$2x + 4y = 8$

$2x + 4(1) = 8$

$2x + 4 = 8$

$2x = 4$

$x = 2$

The solution is **$x = 2$ and $y = 1$**, or the point **(2,1)**.

18. Start by building an equation. David's amount will be d, Jesse's amount will be j, and Mark's amount will be m. All three must add up to $100:

$$d + j + m = 100$$

It may seem like there are three unknowns in this situation, but you can express j and m in terms of d:

Jesse gets $10 less than David, so $j = d - 10$. Mark gets $15 less than Jesse, so $m = j - 15$.

Substitute the previous expression for j to solve for m in terms of d:

$$m = (d - 10) - 15 = d - 25$$

Now back to our original equation, substituting for j and m:

$$d + (d - 10) + (d - 25) = 100$$

$$3d - 35 = 100$$

$$3d = 135$$

$$d = 45$$

David will get **$45**.

19. Start by building an equation. One of the numbers in question will be x. The three numbers are consecutive, so if x is the smallest number then the other two numbers must be $(x + 1)$ and $(x + 2)$. You know that the sum of the three numbers is 54:

$$x + (x + 1) + (x + 2) = 54$$

Now solve for the equation to find x:

$$3x + 3 = 54$$

$$3x = 51$$

$$x = 17$$

The question asks about the middle number $(x + 1)$, so the answer is **18**.

Notice that you could have picked any number to be x. If you picked the middle number as x, your equation would be $(x - 1) + x + (x + 1) = 54$. Solve for x to get 18.

20. This word problem might seem complicated at first, but as long as you keep your variables straight and translate the words into mathematical operations you can easily build an equation. The quantity you want to solve is the number of girls on the swim team, so this will be x.

The number of boys on the swim team will be y. There are 6 fewer boys than girls so $y = x - 6$.

The total number of boys and girls on the swim team is $x + y$.

42 is 8 more than half this number, so $42 = 8 + (x + y) \div 2$

Now substitute for y to solve for x:

$$42 = 8 + (x + x - 6) \div 2$$

$$34 = (2x - 6) \div 2$$

$$68 = 2x - 6$$

$$74 = 2x$$

$$x = 37$$

There are 37 girls on the swim team.

21. Collect like terms on each side as you would for a regular equation:

$$-7x + 2 < 6 - 5x \rightarrow$$

$$-2x < 4$$

When you divide by a negative number, the direction of the sign switches:

$$-2x < 4 = \boldsymbol{x > -2}$$

22. To rearrange the inequality into $y = mx + b$ form, first subtract 4 from both sides:

$$-3x - 4 \geq -y$$

Next divide both sides by -1 to get positive y; remember to switch the direction of the inequality symbol:

$$3x + 4 \leq y$$

Now plot the line $y = 3x + 4$, making a solid line:

Finally, shade the side above the line:

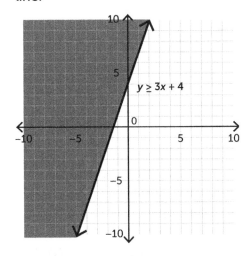

$y \geq 3x + 4$

23. Not every quadratic equation you see will be presented in the standard form. Rearrange terms to set one side equal to 0:

$2x^2 + 14x = 0$

Note that $a = 2$, $b = 14$, and $c = 0$ because there is no third term.

Now divide the expression on the left by the common factor:

$(2x)(x + 7) = 0$

To find the roots, set each of the factors equal to 0:

$2x = 0 \rightarrow x = \mathbf{0}$

$x + 7 = 0 \rightarrow x = \mathbf{-7}$

24. First rearrange the equation to set one side equal to 0:

$3x^2 - 7x + 2 = 0$

Next identify the terms a, b, and c:

$a = 3$, $b = -7$, $c = 2$

Now plug those terms into the quadratic formula:

$x = \dfrac{-b \pm \sqrt{b^2 - 4ac}}{2a}$

$x = \dfrac{7 \pm \sqrt{(-7)^2 - 4(3)(2)}}{2(3)}$

$x = \dfrac{7 \pm \sqrt{25}}{6}$

$x = \dfrac{7 \pm 5}{6}$

Since the determinant is positive, you can expect two real numbers for x. Solve for the two possible answers:

$x = \dfrac{7 + 5}{6} \rightarrow \mathbf{x = 2}$

$x = \dfrac{7 - 5}{6} \rightarrow \mathbf{x = \dfrac{1}{3}}$

25. First, find the axis of symmetry. The equation for the line of symmetry is $x = \dfrac{-b}{2a}$.

$x = \dfrac{-4}{2(1)} = -2$

Next, plug in -2 for x to find the y coordinate of the vertex:

$y = (-2)^2 + 4(-2) + 1 = -3$

The vertex is $(-2, -3)$.

Now, make a table of points on either side of the vertex by plugging in numbers for x and solving for y:

x	$y = x^2 + 4x + 1$	(x, y)
-3	$y = (-3)^2 + 4(-3)$ $+ 1 = -2$	$(-3, -2)$
-1	$y = (-1)^2 + 4(-1)$ $+ 1 = -2$	$(-1, -2)$
-4	$y = (-4)^2 + 4(-4)$ $+ 1 = 1$	$(-4, 1)$
0	$y = 0^2 + 4(0)$ $+ 1 = 1$	$(0, 1)$

Finally, draw the axis of symmetry, plot the vertex and your table of points, and trace the parabola:

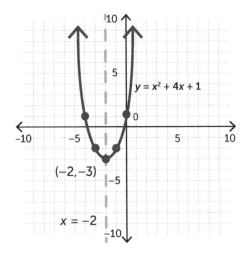

$y = x^2 + 4x + 1$

$(-2, -3)$

$x = -2$

26. Plug in 9 for x:

$f(9) = 2(9) - 10$

$f(9) = 8$

27. The function $f(x)$ has a range of only positive numbers, since x cannot be negative. The function $g(x)$ has a range of positive and negative numbers, since x can be either positive or negative.

The number −2, therefore, must be in the range for $g(x)$ but not for $f(x)$.

28. First, estimate the shape and direction of the graph based on the value of a. Since $a > 1$, you know that $f(x)$ will approach infinity as x increases and there will be a horizontal asymptote along the negative x-axis.

Next, plot the points (0, 1) and (1, a).

Finally, plug in one or two more values for x, plot those points and trace the graph:

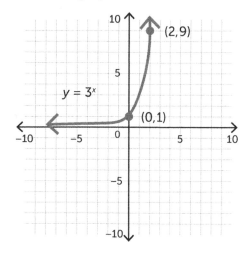

$f(2) = 3^2 = 9 \rightarrow (2, 9)$

29. $64 = 2^x$

The inverse of an exponent is a log. Take the log of both sides to solve for x:

$\log_2 64 = x$

$x = 6$

30. First, estimate the shape and direction of the graph based on the value of a. Since $a > 1$, you know that $f(x)$ will approach infinity as x increases and there will be a vertical asymptote along the negative y-axis.

Next, plot the points (1,0) and (a,1).

Finally, it is easier to plug in a value for $f(x)$ and solve for x rather than attempting to solve for $f(x)$. Plug in one or two values for $f(x)$, plot those points and trace the graph:

$2 = \log_4 x$

$4^2 = x$

$16 = x \rightarrow (16,2)$

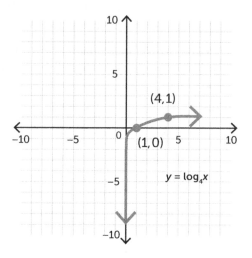

31. Rewrite the function in exponent form:

$x = \frac{1}{3}^{f(x)}$

$81 = \frac{1}{3}^{f(x)}$

The question is asking: to what power must you raise $\frac{1}{3}$ to get 81?

Recognize that $3^4 = 81$,

so $\frac{1}{3}^4 = \frac{1}{81}$

Switch the sign of the exponent to flip the numerator and denominator:

$$\frac{1}{3}^{-4} = \frac{81}{1}$$

$f(81) = -4$

32. Find the difference between two terms that are next to each other:

$$5 - (-1) = -6$$

The common difference is –6. (It must be negative to show the difference is subtracted, not added.)

Now subtract 6 from the last term to find the next term:

$$-13 - 6 = -19$$

The next term is –19.

33. First, decide whether this is an arithmetic or geometric sequence. Since the numbers are getting farther and farther apart, you know this must be a geometric sequence.

Divide one term by the term before it to find the common ratio:

$$18 \div 6 = 3$$

Next, plug in the common ratio and the first term to the equation $a_n = a_1(r^n)$:

$$a_{12} = 2(3^{12})$$

$a_{12} = 1{,}062{,}882$

Notice that it would have taken a very long time to multiply each term by 3 until you got the 12th term – this is where that equation comes in handy!

34. To answer this question, you can simply add 9 + 11 = 20 to get the 5th term, 20 + 11 = 31 to get the 6th term, and so on until you get the 10th term. Or you can plug the information you know into your equation $a_n = a_1 + (n-1)d$. In this

case, you do not know the first term. If you use the fourth term instead, you must replace $(n - 1)$ with $(n - 4)$:

$$a_{10} = 9 + (10 - 4)11$$

$a_{10} = 75$

35. Set up the first equation by removing the absolute value symbol then solve for x:

$$|2x - 3| = x + 1$$
$$2x - 3 = x + 1$$
$$x = 4$$

For the second equation, remove the absolute value and multiply by –1:

$$|2x - 3| = x + 1 \rightarrow$$
$$2x - 3 = -(x + 1) \rightarrow$$
$$2x - 3 = -x - 1 \rightarrow$$
$$3x = 2$$
$$x = \frac{2}{3}$$

Both answers are correct, so the complete answer is **$x = 4$ or $\frac{2}{3}$.**

36. Set up the first equation:

$$2(y + 4) = 10$$
$$y + 4 = 5$$
$$y = 1$$

Set up the second equation. Remember to isolate the absolute value before multiplying by –1:

$$2|y + 4| = 10 \rightarrow$$
$$|y + 4| = 5 \rightarrow$$
$$y + 4 = -5$$
$$y = -9$$

$y = 1$ or –9

37. Start by listing all the data and defining the variable:

total number of backpacks = 48

cost of backpacks = $476.00

backpacks sold in store at price of $18 = 17

backpacks sold to school at a price of $15 = 48 − 17 = 31

total profit = x

Now set up an equation:

income − cost = total profit

$(306 + 465) − 476 = 295$

The store owner made a profit of **$295**.

38. Start by listing all the data and defining your variables. Note that the number of students, while given in the problem, is not needed to find the answer:

time on 1st day = $\frac{3}{5}$ hr. = 36 min.

time on 2nd day = $\frac{1}{2}(36)$ = 18 min.

total time = x

Now set up the equation and solve:

total time = time on 1st day + time on 2nd day

$x = 36 + 18 = 54$

The students had **54 minutes** to work on the projects.

39. The first step is to set up a table and fill in a value for each variable:

	d	r	t
driving	d	30	t
flying	150 − d	60	3 − t

You can now set up equations for driving and flying. The first row gives the equation $d = 30t$ and the second row gives the equation $150 − d = 60(3 − t)$.

Next, solve this system of equations. Start by substituting for d in the second equation:

$d = 30t$

$150 − d = 60(3 − t) \rightarrow 150 − 30t = 60(3 − t)$

Now solve for t:

$150 − 30t = 180 − 60t$

$−30 = −30t$

$1 = t$

Although you've solved for t, you're not done yet. Notice that the problem asks for distance. So, you need to solve for d: what the problem asked for. It does not ask for time, but you need to calculate it to solve the problem.

Driving: $30t = 30$ miles

Flying: $150 − d = 120$ miles

The distance from the airport to the hospital is 120 miles.

40. First, set up the table. The variable for time will be the same for each, because they will have been on the field for the same amount of time when they meet:

	d	r	t
horse #1	d	14	t
horse #2	45 − d	16	t

Next set up two equations:

Horse #1: $d = 14t$

Horse #2: $45 − d = 16t$

Now substitute and solve:

$d = 14t$

$45 − d = 16t \rightarrow 45 − 14t = 16t$

$45 = 30t$

$t = 1.5$

They will meet 1.5 hr. after they begin.

41. Start by figuring out how much of a house each sibling can clean on his or her own. Bridget can clean the house in 12 hours, so she can clean $\frac{1}{12}$ of the house in an hour.

Using the same logic, Tom can clean $\frac{1}{8}$ of a house in an hour.

By adding these values together, you get the fraction of the house they can clean together in an hour:

$\frac{1}{12} + \frac{1}{8} = \frac{5}{24}$

They can do $\frac{5}{24}$ of the job per hour.

Now set up variables and an equation to solve:

t = time spent cleaning (in hours)

h = number of houses cleaned = 2

work = rate × time

$h = \frac{5}{24}t \rightarrow$

$2 = \frac{5}{24}t \rightarrow$

$t = \frac{48}{5} = \mathbf{9\frac{3}{5}}$ **hr.**

42. In this problem you don't know the exact time, but you can still find the hourly rate as a variable:

The first hose completes the job in f hours, so it waters $\frac{1}{f}$ field per hour. The slow hose waters the field in $1.25f$, so it waters the field in $\frac{1}{1.25f}$ hours. Together, they take 5 hours to water the field, so they water $\frac{1}{5}$ of the field per hour.

Now you can set up the equations and solve:

$\frac{1}{f} + \frac{1}{1.25f} = \frac{1}{5} \rightarrow$

$1.25f(\frac{1}{f} + \frac{1}{1.25f}) = 1.25f(\frac{1}{5}) \rightarrow$

$1.25 + 1 = 0.25f$

$2.25 = 0.25f$

$f = 9$

The fast hose takes 9 hours to water the field. The slow hose takes 1.25(9) = **11.25 hours**.

43. Calculate how many apples each person can pick per hour:

Ben: $\frac{500 \text{ apples}}{2 \text{ hr.}} = \frac{250 \text{ apples}}{\text{hr.}}$

Frank: $\frac{450 \text{ apples}}{3 \text{ hr.}} = \frac{150 \text{ apples}}{\text{hr.}}$

Together: $\frac{250 + 150 \text{ apples}}{\text{hr.}} = \frac{400 \text{ apples}}{\text{hr.}}$

Now set up an equation to find the time it takes to pick 1000 apples:

total time $= \frac{1 \text{ hr.}}{400 \text{ apples}} \times 1000$

apples $= \frac{1000}{400 \text{ hr.}} = \mathbf{2.5 \text{ hours}}$

CHAPTER FIVE

Geometry

Properties of Shapes
AREA and PERIMETER

AREA and **PERIMETER** problems require you to use the equations shown in the table below to find either the area inside a shape or the distance around it (the perimeter). These equations will not be given on the test, so you need to have them memorized on test day.

Table 5.1. Area and Perimeter Equations		
SHAPE	AREA	PERIMETER
circle	$A = \pi r^2$	$C = 2\pi r = \pi d$
triangle	$A = \dfrac{b \times h}{2}$	$P = s_1 + s_2 + s_3$
square	$A = s^2$	$P = 4s$
rectangle	$A = l \times w$	$P = 2l + 2w$

EXAMPLES

1. A farmer has purchased 100 meters of fencing to enclose his rectangular garden. If one side of the garden is 20 meters long and the other is 28 meters long, how much fencing will the farmer have left over?

2. Taylor is going to paint a square wall that is 3.5 meters high. How much paint will he need?

VOLUME

Volume is the amount of space taken up by a three-dimensional object. Different formulas are used to find the volumes of different shapes.

Table 5.2. Volume Formulas

Shape	Volume
cylinder	$V = \pi r^2 h$
pyramid	$V = \frac{l \times w \times h}{3}$
cone	$V = \frac{\pi r^2 h}{3}$
sphere	$V = \frac{4}{3}\pi r3$

EXAMPLES

3. Charlotte wants to fill her circular swimming pool with water. The pool has a diameter of 6 meters and is 1 meter deep. How many cubic meters of water will she need to fill the pool?

4. Danny has a fishbowl that is filled to the brim with water, and purchased some spherical glass marbles to line the bottom of it. He dropped in four marbles, and water spilled out of the fishbowl. If the radius of each marble is 1 centimeter, how much water spilled?

CIRCLES

The definition of a circle is the set of points that are equal distance from a center point. The distance from the center to any given point on the circle is the **RADIUS**. If you draw a straight line segment across the circle going through the center, the distance along the line segment from one side of the circle to the other is called the **DIAMETER**. The radius is always equal to half the diameter: $d = 2r$.

DID YOU KNOW?
The equation for a circle on the coordinate plane is $(x - h)^2 + (y - k)^2 = r^2$ where (h,k) is the center of the circle and r is the radius.

A **CENTRAL ANGLE** is formed by drawing radii out from the center to two points A and B along the circle. The **INTERCEPTED ARC** is the portion of the circle (the arc length) between points A and B. You can find the intercepted arc length l if you know the central angle θ and vice versa:

$$l = 2\pi r \frac{\theta}{360°}$$

A **CHORD** is a line segment that connects two points on a circle. Unlike the diameter, a chord does not have to go through the center. You can find the chord length if you know either the central angle θ or the radius of the circle r and the distance from the center of the circle to the chord d (d must be at a right angle to the chord):

If you know the central angle, chord length = $2r\sin\frac{\theta}{2}$

If you know the radius and distance, chord length = $2\sqrt{r^2 - d^2}$

A SECANT is similar to a chord; it connects two points on a circle. The difference is that a secant is a line, not a line segment, so it extends outside of the circle on either side.

A TANGENT is a straight line that touches a circle at only one point.

A SECTOR is the area within a circle that is enclosed by a central angle; if a circle is a pie, a sector is the piece of pie cut by two radii. You can find the AREA OF A SECTOR if you know either the central angle θ or the arc length s.

If you know the central angle, the area of the sector = $\pi r^2 \frac{\theta}{360°}$

If you know the arc length, the area of a sector = $\frac{1}{2}rl$

There are two other types of angles you can create in or around a circle. INSCRIBED ANGLES are *inside* the circle: the vertex is a point P on the circle and the rays extend to two other points on the circle (A and B). As long as A and B remain constant, you can move the vertex P anywhere along the circle and the inscribed angle will be the same. CIRCUMSCRIBED ANGLES are *outside* of the circle: the rays are formed by two tangent lines that touch the circle at points A and B.

You can find the inscribed angle if you know the radius of the circle r and the arc length l between A and B:

$$\text{inscribed angle} = \frac{90°l}{\pi r}$$

To find the circumscribed angle, find the central angle formed by the same points A and B and subtract that angle from 180°.

EXAMPLES

5. A circle has a diameter of 10 centimeters. What is the intercepted arc length between points A and B if the central angle between those points measures 46°?

6. A chord is formed by line segment $\overline{QP}$. The radius of the circle is 5 cm and the chord length is 6 cm. Find the distance from center C to the chord.

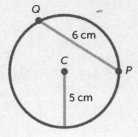

Congruence

CONGRUENCE means having the same size and shape. Two shapes are congruent if you can turn (rotate), flip (reflect), and/or slide (translate) one to fit perfectly on top of the other. Two angles are congruent if they measure the same number of degrees; they do not have to face the same direction nor must they necessarily have rays of equal length. If two triangles have one of the combinations of congruent sides and/or angles listed below, then those triangles are congruent:

- ▶ **SSS** – side, side, side
- ▶ **ASA** – angle, side, angle
- ▶ **SAS** – side, angle, side
- ▶ **AAS** – angle, angle, side

There are a number of common sets of congruent angles in geometry. An ISOSCELES TRIANGLE has two sides of equal length (called the legs) and two congruent angles. If you bisect an isosceles triangle by drawing a line perpendicular to the third side (called the base), you will form two congruent right triangles.

Where two lines cross and form an *X*, the opposite angles are congruent and are called VERTICAL ANGLES. PARALLEL LINES are lines that never cross; if you cut two parallel lines by a transversal, you will form four pairs of congruent CORRESPONDING ANGLES.

A PARALLELOGRAM is a quadrilateral in which both pairs of opposite sides are parallel and congruent (of equal length). In a parallelogram, the two pairs of opposite angles are also congruent. If you divide a parallelogram by either of the diagonals, you will form two congruent triangles.

EXAMPLES

7. Kate and Emily set out for a bike ride together from their house. They ride 6 miles north, then Kate turns 30° to the west and Emily turns 30° to the east. They both ride another 8 miles. If Kate rides 12 miles to return home, how far must Emily ride to get home?

8. Angle *A* measures 53°. Find angle *H*.

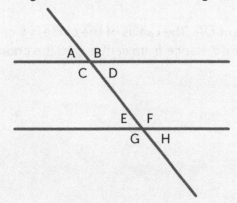

Right Triangles and Trigonometry
PYTHAGOREAN THEOREM

Shapes with 3 sides are known as TRIANGLES. In addition to knowing the formulas for their area and perimeter, you should also know the Pythagorean Theorem, which describes the relationship between the three sides (*a*, *b*, and *c*) of a triangle:

$$a^2 + b^2 = c^2$$

EXAMPLE

9. Erica is going to run a race in which she'll run 3 miles due north and 4 miles due east. She'll then run back to the starting line. How far will she run during this race?

TRIGONOMETRY

Using TRIGONOMETRY, you can calculate an angle in a right triangle based on the ratio of two sides of that triangle. You can also calculate one of the side lengths using the measure of an angle and another side. SINE (SIN), COSINE (COS), and TANGENT (TAN) correspond to the three possible ratios of side lengths. They are defined below:

$$\sin \theta = \frac{opposite}{hypotenuse} \qquad \cos \theta = \frac{adjacent}{hypotenuse} \qquad \tan \theta = \frac{opposite}{adjacent}$$

Opposite is the side opposite from the angle θ, *adjacent* is the side adjacent to the angle θ, and *hypotenuse* is the longest side of the triangle, opposite from the right angle. SOH-CAH-TOA is an acronym to help you remember which ratio goes with which function.

When solving for a side or an angle in a right triangle, first identify which function to use based on the known lengths or angle.

EXAMPLES

10. Phil is hanging holiday lights. To do so safely, he must lean his 20-foot ladder against the outside of his house at an angle of 15° or less. How far from the house can he safely place the base of the ladder?

11. Grace is practicing shooting hoops. She is 5 feet 4 inches tall; her basketball hoop is 10 feet high. From 8 feet away, at what angle does she have to look up to see the hoop? Assume that her eyes are 4 inches lower than the top of her head.

Coordinate Geometry

Coordinate geometry is the study of points, lines, and shapes that have been graphed on a set of axes.

POINTS, LINES, and PLANES

In coordinate geometry, points are plotted on a **COORDINATE PLANE**, a two-dimensional plane in which the **x-AXIS** indicates horizontal direction and the **y-AXIS** indicates vertical direction. The intersection of these two axes is the **ORIGIN**. Points are defined by their location in relation to the horizontal and vertical axes. The coordinates of a point are written **(x, y)**. The coordinates of the origin are $(0, 0)$. The x-coordinates to the right of the origin and the y-coordinates above it are positive; the x-coordinates to the left of the origin and the y-coordinates below it are negative.

A **LINE** is formed by connecting any two points on a coordinate plane; lines are continuous in both directions. Lines can be defined by their **SLOPE**, or steepness, and their **y-INTERCEPT**, or the point at which they intersect the y-axis. A line is represented by the equation $y = mx + b$. The constant m represents slope and the constant b represents the y-intercept.

EXAMPLES

12. Matt parks his car near a forest where he goes hiking. From his car he hikes 1 mile north, 2 miles east, then 3 miles west. If his car represents the origin, find the coordinates of Matt's current location.

13. A square is drawn on a coordinate plane. The bottom corners are located at (−2,3) and (4,3). What are the coordinates for the top right corner?

THE DISTANCE and MIDPOINT FORMULAS

To determine the distance between the points (x_1, y_1) and (x_2, y_2) from a grid use the formula:

$$d = \sqrt{(x_2 - x_1)^2 + (y_2 - y_1)^2}$$

The midpoint, which is halfway between the 2 points, is the point:

$$\left(\frac{x_1 + x_2}{2}, \frac{y_1 + y_2}{2} \right)$$

EXAMPLES

14. What is the distance between points (3,−6) and (−5,2)?

15. What is the midpoint between points (3,−6) and (−5,2)?

Answer Key

1. The perimeter of a rectangle is equal to twice its length plus twice its width:

   $P = 2(20) + 2(28) = 96$ m

   The farmer has 100 meters of fencing, so he'll have
   $100 - 96 = $ **4 meters** left.

2. Each side of the square wall is 3.5 meters:

   $A = 3.5^2 = $ **12.25m²**

3. This question is asking about the volume of Charlotte's pool. The circular pool is actually a cylinder, so use the formula for a cylinder:
   $V = \pi r^2 h$.

   The diameter is 6 meters. The radius is half the diameter so
   $r = 6 \div 2 = 3$ meters.

   Now solve for the volume:

   $V = \pi r^2 h$

   $V = \pi (3 \text{ m})^2 (1 \text{ m})$

   $V = 28.3 \text{ m}^3$

   Charlotte will need approximately **28.3 cubic meters** of water to fill her pool.

4. Since the fishbowl was filled to the brim, the volume of the water that spilled out of it is equal to the volume of the marbles that Danny dropped into it. First, find the volume of one marble using the equation for a sphere:

   $V = \frac{4}{3}\pi r^3$

   $V = \frac{4}{3}\pi (1 \text{ cm})^3$

   $V = 4.2 \text{ cm}^3$

   Since Danny dropped in 4 marbles, multiply this volume by 4 to find the total volume:

   $4.2 \text{ cm}^3 \times 4 = 16.8 \text{ cm}^3$

   Approximately **16.8 cubic centimeters** of water spilled out of the fishbowl.

5. First divide the diameter by two to find the radius:

   $r = 10 \text{ cm} \div 2 = 5 \text{ cm}$

   Now use the formula for intercepted arc length:

   $l = 2\pi r \frac{\theta}{360°}$

   $l = 2\pi (5 \text{ cm})\frac{46°}{360°}$

   $l = $ **4.0 cm**

6. Use the formula for chord length:

   chord length $= 2\sqrt{r^2 - d^2}$

   In this example, we are told the chord length and the radius, and we need to solve for d:

   $6 \text{ cm} = 2\sqrt{(5 \text{ cm})^2 - d^2}$

   $3 \text{ cm} = \sqrt{(5 \text{ cm})^2 - d^2}$

   $9 \text{ cm}^2 = 25 \text{ cm}^2 - d^2$

   $d^2 = 16 \text{ cm}^2$

   $d = $ **4 cm**

7. Draw out Kate's and Emily's trips to see that their routes form two triangles. The triangles have corresponding sides with lengths of 6 miles and 8 miles, and a corresponding angle in between of 150°. This fits the "SAS" rule so the triangles must be congruent. The length Kate has to ride home corresponds to the length Emily has to ride home, so **Emily must ride 12 miles.**

8. For parallel lines cut by a transversal, look for vertical and corresponding angles.

Angles A and D are vertical angles, so angle D must be congruent to angle A. Angle D = 53°.

Angles D and H are corresponding angles, so angle H must be congruent to angle D. **Angle H = 53°.**

9. Start by drawing a picture of Erica's route. You'll see it forms a triangle:

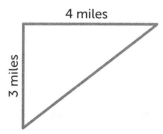

One leg of the triangle is missing, but you can find its length using the Pythagorean Theorem:

$a^2 + b^2 = c^2$

$3^2 + 4^2 = c^2$

$25 = c^2$

$c = 5$

Adding all 3 sides gives the length of the whole race:

$3 + 4 + 5 =$ **12 miles**

10. Draw a triangle with the known length and angle labeled.

The known side (the length of the ladder) is the hypotenuse of the triangle, and the unknown distance is the side opposite the angle. Therefore, you can use sine:

$\sin\theta = \frac{opposite}{hypotenuse}$

$\sin 15° = \frac{opposite}{20 \text{ feet}}$

Now solve for the opposite side:

$opposite = \sin 15° (20 \text{ feet})$

$opposite =$ **5.2 feet**

11. Draw a diagram and notice that the line from Grace's eyes to the hoop of the basket forms the hypotenuse of a right triangle. The side adjacent to the angle of her eyes is the distance from the basket: 8 feet. The side opposite to Grace's eyes is the difference between the height of her eyes and the height of the basket: 10 feet – 5 feet = 5 feet.

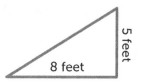

Next, use the formula for tangent to solve for the angle:

$\tan\theta = \frac{opposite}{adjacent}$

$\tan\theta = \frac{5 \text{ ft}}{8 \text{ ft}}$

Now take the inverse tangent of both sides to solve for the angle:

$\theta = \tan^{-1}\frac{5}{8}$

$\theta =$ **32°**

12. To find the coordinates, you must find Matt's displacement along the x- and y-axes. Matt hiked 1 mile north and zero miles south, so his displacement along the y-axis is +1 mile. Matt hiked 2

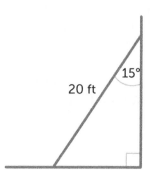

miles east and 3 miles west, so his displacement along the x-axis is + 2 miles – 3 miles = –1 mile.

Matt's coordinates are (–1,1).

13. Draw the coordinate plane and plot the given points. If you connect these points you will see that the bottom side is 6 units long. Since it is a square, all sides must be 6 units long. Count 6 units up from the point (4,3) to find the top right corner.

The coordinates for the top right corner are (4,9).

14. Plug the values for $x_1, x_2, y_1,$ and y_2 into the distance formula and simplify:

$$d = \sqrt{(-5-3)^2 + (2-(-6))^2} =$$
$$\sqrt{64+64} = \sqrt{64 \times 2} = \mathbf{8\sqrt{2}}$$

15. Plug the values for $x_1, x_2, y_1,$ and y_2 into the midpoint formula and simplify:

$$midpoint = \left(\frac{3+(-5)}{2}, \frac{(-6)+2}{2}\right)$$
$$= \left(\frac{-2}{2}, \frac{-4}{2}\right) = \mathbf{(-1,-2)}$$

CHAPTER SIX

Statistics and Probability

Describing Sets of Data

STATISTICS is the study of sets of data. The goal of statistics is to take a group of values—numerical answers from a survey, for example—and look for patterns in how that data is distributed.

When looking at a set of data, it's helpful to consider the **MEASURES OF CENTRAL TENDENCY**, a group of values that describe the central or typical data point from the set. The SAT covers three measures of central tendency: mean, median, and mode.

MEAN is the mathematical term for *average*. To find the mean, total all the terms and divide by the number of terms. The **MEDIAN** is the middle number of a given set. To find the median, put the terms in numerical order; the middle number will be the median. In the case of a set of even numbers, the middle two numbers are averaged. **MODE** is the number which occurs most frequently within a given set. If two different numbers both appear with the highest frequency, they are both the mode.

When examining a data set, also consider **MEASURES OF VARIABILITY**, which describe how the data is dispersed around the central data point. The SAT covers two measures of variability: range and standard deviation. **RANGE** is simply the difference between the largest and smallest values in the set. **STANDARD DEVIATION** is a measure of how dispersed the data is, or how far it reaches from the mean.

EXAMPLES

1. Find the mean of 24, 27, and 18.

2. The mean of three numbers is 45. If two of the numbers are 38 and 43, what is the third number?

3. What is the median of 24, 27, and 18?

4. What is the median of 24, 27, 18, and 19?

5. What is the mode of 2, 5, 4, 4, 3, 2, 8, 9, 2, 7, 2, and 2?

6. What is the standard deviation of 62, 63, 61, and 66?

Graphs and Charts

These questions require you to interpret information from graphs and charts; they are pretty straightforward as long as you pay careful attention to detail. There are several different graph and chart types that may appear on the SAT.

BAR GRAPHS

BAR GRAPHS present the numbers of an item that exist in different categories. The categories are shown on the *x*-axis, and the number of items is shown on the *y*-axis. Bar graphs are usually used to easily compare amounts.

EXAMPLES

7. The chart below shows rainfall in inches per month. Which month had the least amount of rainfall? Which had the most?

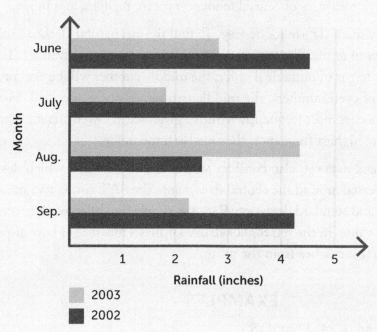

8. Using the chart below, how many more ice cream cones were sold in July than in September?

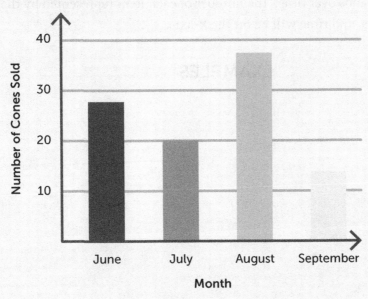

PIE CHARTS

PIE CHARTS present parts of a whole, and are often used with percentages. Together, all the slices of the pie add up to the total number of items, or 100%.

EXAMPLES

9. The pie chart below shows the distribution of birthdays in a class of students. How many students have birthdays in the spring or summer?

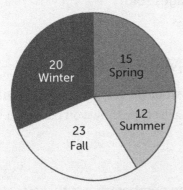

Distribution of Students' Birthdays

10. Using the same graph above, what percentage of students have birthdays in winter?

LINE GRAPHS

LINE GRAPHS show trends over time. The number of each item represented by the graph will be on the *y*-axis, and time will be on the *x*-axis.

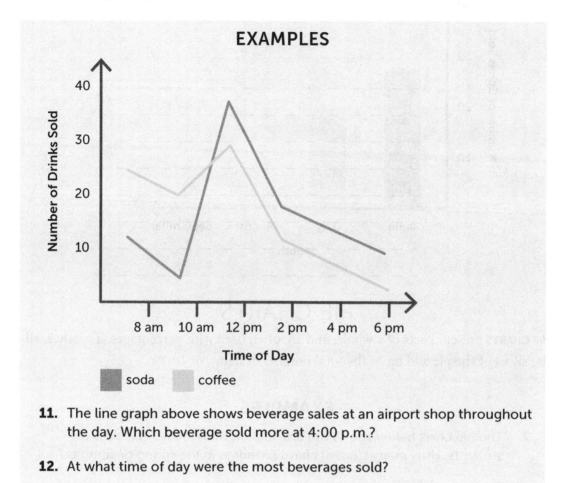

EXAMPLES

11. The line graph above shows beverage sales at an airport shop throughout the day. Which beverage sold more at 4:00 p.m.?

12. At what time of day were the most beverages sold?

HISTOGRAMS

A HISTOGRAM shows a distribution of types within a whole in bar chart form. While they look like bar graphs, they are more similar to pie charts: they show you parts of a whole.

EXAMPLE

13. The chart on the following page shows the number of cars that traveled through a toll plaza throughout the day. How many cars passed through the toll plaza between 8:00 a.m. and 5:00 p.m.?

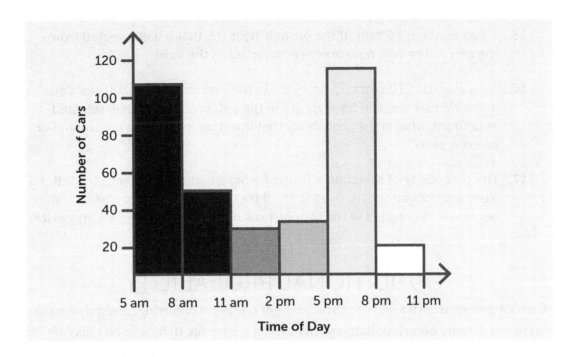

Probability

PROBABILITY is the likelihood that an event will take place. This likelihood is expressed as a value between 0 and 1. The closer the probability is to zero, the less likely the event is to occur; the closer the probability is to 1, the more likely it is to occur.

PROBABILITY of a SINGLE EVENT

The probability of an outcome occurring is found by dividing the number of desired outcomes by the number of total possible outcomes. As with percentages, a probability is the ratio of a part to a whole, with the whole being the total number of possibilities, and the part being the number of desired results. Probabilities can be written using percentages (40%), decimals (0.4), fractions, or in words (the probability of an outcome is 2 in 5).

$$\text{probability} = \frac{\text{desired outcomes}}{\text{total possible outcomes}}$$

EXAMPLES

14. A bag holds 3 blue marbles, 5 green marbles, and 7 red marbles. If you pick one marble from the bag, what is the probability it will be blue?

15. A bag contains 75 balls. If the probability is 0.6 that a ball selected from the bag will be red, how many red balls are in the bag?

16. A theater has 230 seats: 75 seats are in the orchestra area, 100 seats are in the mezzanine, and 55 seats are in the balcony. If a ticket is selected at random, what is the probability that it will be for either a mezzanine or balcony seat?

17. The probability of selecting a student whose name begins with the letter *S* from a school attendance log is 7%. If there are 42 students whose names begin with *S* enrolled at the school, how many students in total attend it?

CONDITIONAL PROBABILITY

CONDITIONAL PROBABILITY refers to the chances of one event occurring, given that another event has already occurred. **INDEPENDENT EVENTS** are events that have no effect on one another. The classic example is flipping a coin: whether you flip heads or tails one time has no bearing on how you might flip the next time. Your chance of flipping heads is always 50/50. **DEPENDENT EVENTS**, on the other hand, have an effect on the next event's probability. If you have a bag full of red and blue marbles, removing a red marble the first time will decrease the probability of picking a red marble the second time, since now there are fewer red marbles in the bag. The probability of event *B* occurring, given that event *A* has occurred, is written $P(B|A)$.

The probability of either event *A* or event *B* occurring is called the **UNION** of events *A* and *B*, written $A \cup B$. The probability of $A \cup B$ is equal to the <u>sum</u> of the probability of *A* occurring and the probability of *B* occurring, <u>minus</u> the probability of both *A* and *B* occurring. The probability of both *A* and *B* occurring is called the **INTERSECTION** of events *A* and *B*, written $A \cap B$. The probability of $A \cap B$ is equal to the <u>product</u> of the probability of *A* and the probability of *B*, given *A*. Review the equations for the probabilities of unions and intersections below:

$$P(A \cup B) = P(A) + P(B) - P(A \cap B)$$
$$P(A \cap B) = P(A) \times P(B|A)$$

The **COMPLEMENT** of an event is when the event <u>does not</u> occur. The probability of the complement of event *A*, written $P(A')$, is equal to $1 - P(A)$.

EXAMPLES

18. A bag contains 5 red marbles and 11 blue marbles. What is the probability of pulling out a blue marble, followed by a red marble?

19. Caroline randomly draws a playing card from a full deck. What is the chance she will select either a queen or a diamond?

Answer Key

1. Add the terms, then divide by the number of terms:

   $\text{mean} = \dfrac{24 + 27 + 18}{3} = \mathbf{23}$

2. Set up the equation for mean with x representing the third number, then solve:

   $\text{mean} = \dfrac{38 + 43 + x}{3} = 45$

   $\dfrac{38 + 43 + x}{3} = 45$

   $38 + 43 + x = 135$

   $\mathbf{x = 54}$

3. Place the terms in order, then pick the middle term:

   18, 24, 27

   The median is **24**.

4. Place the terms in order. Because there is an even number of terms, the median will be the average of the middle 2 terms:

   18, 19, 24, 27

   $\text{median} = \dfrac{19 + 24}{2} = \mathbf{21.5}$

5. The mode is **2** because it appears the most within the set.

6. To find the standard deviation, first find the mean:

   $\text{mean} = \dfrac{62 + 63 + 61 + 66}{4} = 63$

   Next, find the difference between each term and the mean, and square that number:

   $63 - 62 = 1 \rightarrow 1^2 = 1$

   $63 - 63 = 0 \rightarrow 0^2 = 0$

   $63 - 61 = 2 \rightarrow 2^2 = 4$

   $63 - 66 = -3 \rightarrow (-3)^2 = 9$

   Now, find the mean of the squares:

   $\text{mean} = \dfrac{1 + 0 + 4 + 9}{4} = 3.5$

   Finally, find the square root of the mean:

   $\sqrt{3.5} = 1.87$

   The standard deviation is **1.87**.

7. The shortest bar will be the month that had the least rain, and the longest bar will correspond to the month with the greatest amount: **July 2003 had the least**, and **June 2002 had the most**.

8. Tracing from the top of each bar to the scale on the left shows that sales in July were 20 and September sales were 15. So, **5 more cones were sold in July**.

9. 15 students have birthdays in the spring and 12 in winter, so there are **27 students** with birthdays in spring or summer.

10. Use the equation for percent:

    $\text{percent} = \dfrac{\text{part}}{\text{whole}} = \dfrac{\text{winter birthdays}}{\text{total birthdays}} \rightarrow$

    $\dfrac{20}{20 + 15 + 23 + 12} = \dfrac{20}{70} = \dfrac{2}{7} = .286$

    or **28.6%**

11. At 4:00 p.m., approximately 12 sodas and 5 coffees were sold, so more **soda** was sold.

12. This question is asking for the time of day with the most sales of coffee and soda combined. It is not necessary to add up sales at each time of day to find the answer. Just from looking at the graph, you can see that sales for both beverages were highest at noon, so the answer must be **12:00 p.m.**

13. To find the total number, we need to add the number of cars for each relevant time period (note that all number are approximations):

8:00 a.m. – 11:00 a.m.: 50 cars

11:00 a.m. – 2:00 p.m.: 30 cars

2:00 p.m. – 5:00 p.m.: 35 cars

50 + 30 + 35 = **115 cars**

14. Because there are 15 marbles in the bag (3 + 5 + 7), the total number of possible outcomes is 15. Of those outcomes, 3 would be blue marbles, which is the desired outcome. Using that information, you can set up an equation:

$$probability = \frac{desired\ outcomes}{total\ possible\ outcomes}$$
$$= \frac{3}{15} = \frac{1}{5}$$

The probability is **1 in 5 or 0.2** that a blue marble is picked.

15. Because you're solving for desired outcomes (the number of red balls), first you need to rearrange the equation:

$$probability = \frac{desired\ outcomes}{total\ possible\ outcomes}$$
$$desired\ outcomes = probability \times total\ possible\ outcomes$$

Here, choosing a red ball is the desired outcome; the total possible outcomes are represented by the 75 total balls.

There are **45 red balls** in the bag.

16. In this problem, the desired outcome is a seat in either the mezzanine or balcony area, and the total possible outcomes are represented by the 230 total seats. So you can write this equation:

$$probability = \frac{desired\ outcomes}{total\ possible\ outcomes}$$
$$= \frac{100 + 55}{230} = \textbf{0.67}$$

17. Because you're solving for total possible outcomes (total number of students), first you need to rearrange the equation:

$$total\ possible\ outcomes = \frac{desired\ outcomes}{probability}$$

In this problem, you are given a probability (7% or 0.07) and the number of desired outcomes (42). Plug these numbers into the equation to solve:

$$total\ possible\ outcomes = \frac{42}{0.07} = \textbf{600 students}$$

18. This question is asking about an intersection of events. The equation for an intersection of events is

$$P(A \cap B) = P(A) \times P(B|A).$$

The first event, event A, is picking out a blue marble. Find $P(A)$:

$$P(A) = \frac{11\ blue\ marbles}{16\ total\ marbles} = \frac{11}{16}$$

The second event, event B, is picking out a red marble, now that there are 15 marbles left. Find $P(B|A)$:

$$P(B|A) = \frac{5\ red\ marbles}{15\ total\ marbles} = \frac{5}{15} = \frac{1}{3}$$
$$P(A \cap B) = P(A) \times P(B|A)$$
$$= \frac{11}{16} \times \frac{1}{3} = \frac{\textbf{11}}{\textbf{48}}$$

19. This question is asking about a union of events. The equation for a union of events is

$$P(A \cup B) = P(A) + P(B) - P(A \cap B).$$

The first event, event A, is selecting a queen. Find $P(A)$:

$$P(A) = \frac{4\ queens}{52\ total\ cards} = \frac{4}{52}$$

The second event, event B, is selecting a diamond. Find $P(B)$:

$$P(B) = \frac{13\ diamonds}{52\ total\ cards} = \frac{13}{52}$$

Now, find the probability of selecting a queen that is also a diamond:

$$P(A \cap B) = \frac{1 \text{ diamond queen}}{52 \text{ total cards}} = \frac{1}{52}$$

$$P(A \cup B) = P(A) + P(B) - P(A \cap B)$$
$$= \frac{4}{52} + \frac{13}{52} - \frac{1}{52} = \frac{16}{52} = \mathbf{\frac{4}{13}}$$

PART III
The Essay
1 prompt ¦ 50 minutes

On the Essay section of the SAT, you'll be required to read a short passage and write an essay analyzing the author's argument. The passage will address an issue from science, art, or civics and provide different viewpoints and a range of supporting evidence. Your job will be to describe how the author presented his or her argument. Your essay should include a discussion of the following:

▶   the author's main argument

▶   the structure of the passage

▶   the evidence the author uses to support his or her claim

▶   the rhetorical elements (e.g., metaphors, word choice, or appeals to emotion and authority) used by the author

You should not discuss your own opinion or reactions to the passage in your essay. Your only task is to objectively analyze the author's argument, not to discuss how you personally feel about either the topic or the effectiveness of the passage.

CHAPTER SEVEN

Writing the Essay

Structuring the Essay

There are a few different ways to organize an essay, but some basics apply no matter what the style.

Essays may differ in how they present an idea, but they all have the same basic parts—introduction, body, and conclusion. The most common essay types are persuasive essays and expository essays. A persuasive essay takes a position on an issue and attempts to show the reader why it is correct. An expository essay explains different aspects of an issue without necessarily taking a side.

INTRODUCTIONS

Present your argument or idea in the introduction. Usually, the introductory paragraph ends with a thesis statement, which clearly sets forth the position or point the essay will prove. The introduction is a good place to bring up complexities, counterarguments, and context, all of which will help the reader understand the reasoning behind your position on the issue at hand. Later, revisit those issues and wrap all of them up in the conclusion.

EXAMPLE

Below is an example of an introduction. Note that it provides some context for the argument, acknowledges an opposing perspective, and gives the reader a good idea of the issue's complexities. Pay attention to the thesis statement in the last few lines, which clearly states the author's position.

Technology has changed immensely in recent years, but today's generation barely notices—high school students are already experienced with the internet, computers, apps, cameras, cell phones, and more. Teenagers must learn to use these tools safely and responsibly. Opponents of 1:1 technology programs might argue that students will be distracted or misuse the technology, but that is exactly why schools must teach them to use it. By providing technology to students, schools can help them apply it positively by creating projects with other students, communicating with teachers and classmates, and conducting research for class projects. In a world where technology is improving and changing at a phenomenal rate, schools have a responsibility to teach students how to navigate that technology safely and effectively; providing each student with a laptop or tablet is one way to help them do that.

THE BODY PARAGRAPHS

The body of an essay consists of a series of structured paragraphs. You may organize the body of your essay by creating paragraphs that describe or explain each reason you give in your thesis; addressing the issue as a problem and offering a solution in a separate paragraph; telling a story that demonstrates your point (make sure to break it into paragraphs around related ideas); or comparing and contrasting the merits of two opposing sides of the issue (make sure to draw a conclusion about which is better at the end).

Make sure that each paragraph is structurally consistent, beginning with a topic sentence to introduce the main idea, followed by supporting ideas and examples. No extra ideas unrelated to the paragraph's focus should appear. Use transition words and phrases to connect body paragraphs and improve the flow and readability of your essay.

In the *Providing Supporting Evidence* section you will find an example of a paragraph that is internally consistent and explains one of the main reasons given in the example introduction that you just read. Your essay should have one or more paragraphs like this to form the main body.

CONCLUSIONS

In order to end your essay smoothly, write a conclusion that reminds the reader why you were talking about these topics in the first place. Go back to the ideas in the introduction and thesis statement, but be careful not to simply restate your ideas; rather, reinforce your argument.

EXAMPLE

Below is a sample conclusion paragraph that could go with the introduction above. Notice that this conclusion talks about the same topics as the introduction (changing technology and the responsibility of schools), but it does not simply rewrite the thesis.

As technology continues to change, teens will need to adapt to it. Schools already teach young people myriad academic and life skills, so it makes sense that they would teach students how to use technology appropriately, too.

Providing students with their own devices is one part of that important task, and schools should be supporting it.

Writing a Thesis Statement

The THESIS, or THESIS STATEMENT, is central to the structure and meaning of an essay. It presents the writer's argument, or position on an issue; in other words, it tells readers specifically what you think and what you will discuss. A strong, direct thesis statement is key to the organization of any essay. The thesis statement is typically located at the end of the introductory paragraph.

Writing a good thesis statement is as simple as stating your idea and why you think it is true or correct.

EXAMPLE

The Prompt

Many high schools have begun to adopt 1:1 technology programs, meaning that each school provides every student with a computing device such as a laptop or tablet. Educators who support these initiatives say that the technology allows for more dynamic collaboration and that students need to learn technology skills to compete in the job market. On the other hand, opponents cite increased distraction and the dangers of cyber-bullying or unsupervised internet use as reasons not to provide students with such devices.

In your essay, take a position on this question. You may write about either one of the two points of view given, or you may present a different point of view on this question. Use specific reasons and examples to support your position.

Possible thesis statements:

Providing technology to every student is good for education because it allows students to learn important skills such as typing, web design, and video editing; it also gives students more opportunities to work cooperatively with their classmates and teachers.

I disagree with the idea that schools should provide technology to students because most students will simply be distracted by the free access to games and websites when they should be studying or doing homework.

In a world where technology is improving and changing at a phenomenal rate, schools have a responsibility to teach students how to navigate that technology safely and effectively; providing each student with a laptop or tablet is one way to help them do that.

Providing Supporting Evidence

Your essay requires not only structured, organized paragraphs; it must also provide specific evidence supporting your arguments. Whenever you make a general statement, follow it with specific examples that will help to convince the reader that your argument has merit. These specific examples do not bring new ideas to the paragraph; rather, they explain or defend the general ideas that have already been stated.

The following are some examples of general statements and specific statements that provide more detailed support:

GENERAL: Students may get distracted online or access harmful websites.

SPECIFIC: Some students spend too much time using chat features or social media, or they get caught up in online games. Others spend time reading websites that have nothing to do with an assignment.

SPECIFIC: Teens often think they are hidden behind their computer screens. If teenagers give out personal information such as age or location on a website, it can lead to dangerous strangers seeking them out.

GENERAL: Schools can teach students how to use technology appropriately and expose them to new tools.

SPECIFIC: Schools can help students learn to use technology to work on class projects, communicate with classmates and teachers, and carry out research for classwork.

SPECIFIC: Providing students with laptops or tablets will allow them to get lots of practice using technology and programs at home, and only school districts can ensure that these tools are distributed widely, especially to students who may not have them at home.

EXAMPLE

Below is an example of a structured paragraph that uses specific supporting ideas. This paragraph supports the thesis introduced above (see Introductions*).*

Providing students with their own laptop or tablet will allow them to explore new programs and software in class with teachers and classmates and to practice using it at home. In schools without laptops for students, classes have to visit computer labs where they share old computers that are often missing keys or that run so slowly they are hardly powered on before class ends. When a teacher tries to show students how to use a new tool or website, students must scramble to follow along and have no time to explore the new feature. If they can take laptops home instead, students can do things like practice editing video clips or photographs until they are perfect. They can email classmates or use shared files to collaborate even after school. If schools expect students to learn these skills, it is the schools' responsibility to provide students with enough opportunities to practice them.

This paragraph has some general statements:

... their own laptop or tablet will allow them to explore new programs and software... and to practice...

...it is the schools' responsibility to provide... enough opportunities...

It also has some specific examples to back them up:

...computers... run so slowly they are hardly powered on... students must scramble to follow along and have no time to explore...

They can email classmates or use shared files to collaborate...

Writing Well
TRANSITIONS

Transitions are words, phrases, and ideas that help connect ideas throughout a text. You should use them between sentences and between paragraphs. Some common transitions include *then, next, in other words, as well, in addition to.* Be creative with your transitions, and make sure you understand what the transition you are using shows about the relationship between the ideas. For instance, the transition *although* implies that there is some contradiction between the first idea and the second.

SYNTAX

The way you write sentences is important to maintaining the reader's interest. Try to begin sentences differently. Make some sentences long and some sentences short. Write simple sentences. Write complex sentences that have complex ideas in them. Readers appreciate variety.

There are four basic types of sentences: simple, compound, complex, and compound-complex. Try to use some of each type. Be sure that your sentences make sense, though—it is better to have clear and simple writing that a reader can understand than to have complex, confusing syntax that does not clearly express the idea.

WORD CHOICE and TONE

The words you choose influence the impression you make on readers. Use words that are specific, direct, and appropriate to the task. For instance, a formal text may benefit from complex sentences and impressive vocabulary, while it may be more appropriate to use simple vocabulary and sentences in writing intended for a young audience. Make use of strong vocabulary; avoid using vague, general words such as *good*, *bad*, *very*, or *a lot*. However, make sure that you are comfortable with the vocabulary you choose; if you are unsure about the word's meaning or its use in the context of your essay, don't use it at all.

EDITING, REVISING, and PROOFREADING

When writing a timed essay, you will not have very much time for these steps; spend any time you have left after writing the essay looking over it and checking for spelling and grammar mistakes that may interfere with a reader's understanding. Common mistakes to look out for include: subject/verb disagreement, pronoun/antecedent disagreement, comma splices and run-ons, and sentence fragments (phrases or dependent clauses unconnected to an independent clause).

Practice Essay

Read the passage from John F. Kennedy's 1963 Commencement Address, and then write an essay based on the prompt.

As you read the passage below, consider how John F. Kennedy uses:

- ▶ evidence, such as facts or examples, to support claims
- ▶ reasoning to develop ideas and to connect claims and evidence
- ▶ stylistic or persuasive elements, such as word choice or appeals to emotion, to add power to the ideas expressed

ADAPTED FROM THE COMMENCEMENT ADDRESS GIVEN BY JOHN F. KENNEDY AT AMERICAN UNIVERSITY ON JUNE 10, 1963.

I have, therefore, chosen this time and place to discuss a topic on which ignorance too often abounds and the truth is too rarely perceived. And that is the most important topic on Earth: peace. What kind of peace do I mean and what kind of a peace do we seek? Not a Pax Americana enforced on the world by American weapons of war. Not the peace of the grave or the security of the slave. I am talking about genuine peace, the kind of peace that makes life on Earth worth living, and the kind that enables men and nations to grow, and to hope, and build a better life for their children; not merely peace for Americans but peace for all men and women, not merely peace in our time but peace in all time.

I speak of peace because of the new face of war. Total war makes no sense in an age where great powers can maintain large and relatively invulnerable nuclear forces and refuse to surrender without resort to those forces. It makes no sense in an age where a single nuclear weapon contains almost ten times the explosive force delivered by all the allied air forces in the Second World War.

It makes no sense in an age when the deadly poisons produced by a nuclear exchange would be carried by wind and water and soil and seed to the far corners of the globe and to generations yet unborn.

Today the expenditure of billions of dollars every year on weapons acquired for the purpose of making sure we never need them is essential to the keeping of peace. But surely the acquisition of such idle stockpiles which can only destroy and never create is not the only, much less the most efficient, means of assuring peace. I speak of peace, therefore, as the necessary, rational end of rational men. I realize the pursuit of peace is not as dramatic as the pursuit of war, and frequently the words of the pursuers fall on deaf ears. But we have no more urgent task.

Some say that it is useless to speak of peace or world law or world disarmament, and that it will be useless until the leaders of the Soviet Union adopt a more enlightened attitude. I hope they do. I believe we can help them do it. But I also believe that we must reexamine our own attitudes, as individuals and as a Nation, for our attitude is as essential as theirs.

And every graduate of this school, every thoughtful citizen who despairs of war and wishes to bring peace, should begin by looking inward, by examining his own attitude towards the possibilities of peace, towards the Soviet Union, towards the course of the Cold War and towards freedom and peace here at home.

First examine our attitude towards peace itself. Too many of us think it is impossible. Too many think it is unreal. But that is a dangerous, defeatist belief. It leads to the conclusion that war is inevitable, that mankind is doomed, that we are gripped by forces we cannot control. We need not accept that view. Our problems are manmade; therefore, they can be solved by man. And man can be as big as he wants.

No problem of human destiny is beyond human beings. Man's reason and spirit have often solved the seemingly unsolvable, and we believe they can do it again. I am not referring to the absolute, infinite concept of universal peace and good will of which some fantasies and fanatics dream. I do not deny the value of hopes and dreams but we merely invite discouragement and incredulity by making that our only and immediate goal.

Let us focus instead on a more practical, more attainable peace, based not on a sudden revolution in human nature but on a gradual evolution in human institutions, on a series of concrete actions and effective agreements which are in the interest of all concerned. There is no single, simple key to this peace; no grand or magic formula to be adopted by one or two powers. Genuine peace must be the product of many nations, the sum of many acts. It must be dynamic, not static, changing to meet the challenge of each new generation. For peace is a process, a way of solving problems.

PROMPT

Write an essay explaining how John F. Kennedy builds his argument to convince his audience that peace between the United States and Soviet Union will come about not through a "Pax Americana" obtained in an American victory in a nuclear war, but through a fundamental shift in the human attitude towards peace. In your essay, explain how he uses the techniques and elements listed above to strengthen his argument; be sure to focus on the most relevant ones. Remember not to discuss whether you agree with Kennedy or not; analyze his argument and explain it to your audience instead.

PART IV
Test Your Knowledge
154 multiple choice questions; 1 essay ¦ 3 hours and 50 minutes

CHAPTER EIGHT
Practice Test

Reading

There are several passages in this test and each passage is accompanied by several questions. After reading a passage, choose the best answer to each question and fill in the corresponding oval on your answer document. You may refer to the passages as often as necessary.

Questions 1 – 10 are based on the following passage, adapted from Nathaniel Hawthorne's short story "The Artist of the Beautiful," originally published in 1844. Owen Warland is a young watchmaker, who studied his trade as an apprentice under retired watchmaker Peter Hovenden.

From the time that his little fingers could grasp a penknife, Owen had been remarkable for a delicate ingenuity, which sometimes produced pretty shapes in wood, principally figures of flowers and birds, and sometimes seemed to aim at the hidden mysteries of mechanism. But it was always for purposes of grace, and never with any mockery of
(5) the useful. He did not, like the crowd of school-boy artisans, construct little windmills on the angle of a barn or watermills across the neighboring brook. Those who discovered such peculiarity in the boy as to think it worth their while to observe him closely, sometimes saw reason to suppose that he was attempting to imitate the beautiful movements of Nature as exemplified in the flight of birds or the activity of little animals.
(10) It seemed, in fact, a new development of the love of the beautiful, such as might have made him a poet, a painter, or a sculptor, and which was as completely refined from all utilitarian coarseness as it could have been in either of the fine arts. He looked with singular distaste at the stiff and regular processes of ordinary machinery. Being once carried to see a steam-engine, in the expectation that his intuitive comprehension of
(15) mechanical principles would be gratified, he turned pale and grew sick, as if something monstrous and unnatural had been presented to him. This horror was partly owing to

the size and terrible energy of the iron laborer; for the character of Owen's mind was microscopic, and tended naturally to the minute, in accordance with his diminutive frame and the marvelous smallness and delicate power of his fingers. Not that his sense (20) of beauty was thereby diminished into a sense of prettiness. The beautiful idea has no relation to size, and may be as perfectly developed in a space too minute for any but microscopic investigation as within the ample verge that is measured by the arc of the rainbow. But, at all events, this characteristic minuteness in his objects and accomplishments made the world even more incapable than it might otherwise have been (25) of appreciating Owen Warland's genius. The boy's relatives saw nothing better to be done—as perhaps there was not—than to bind him apprentice to a watchmaker, hoping that his strange ingenuity might thus be regulated and put to utilitarian purposes.

Peter Hovenden's opinion of his apprentice has already been expressed. He could make nothing of the lad. Owen's apprehension of the professional mysteries, it is true, (30) was inconceivably quick; but he altogether forgot or despised the grand object of a watchmaker's business, and cared no more for the measurement of time than if it had been merged into eternity. So long, however, as he remained under his old master's care, Owen's lack of sturdiness made it possible, by strict injunctions and sharp oversight, to restrain his creative eccentricity within bounds; but when his apprenticeship was served (35) out, and he had taken the little shop which Peter Hovenden's failing eyesight compelled him to relinquish, then did people recognize how unfit a person was Owen Warland to lead old blind Father Time along his daily course. One of his most rational projects was to connect a musical operation with the machinery of his watches, so that all the harsh dissonances of life might be rendered tuneful, and each flitting moment fall (40) into the abyss of the past in golden drops of harmony. If a family clock was entrusted to him for repair,—one of those tall, ancient clocks that have grown nearly allied to human nature by measuring out the lifetime of many generations,—he would take upon himself to arrange a dance or funeral procession of figures across its venerable face, representing twelve mirthful or melancholy hours. Several freaks of this kind quite (45) destroyed the young watchmaker's credit with that steady and matter-of-fact class of people who hold the opinion that time is not to be trifled with, whether considered as the medium of advancement and prosperity in this world or preparation for the next. His custom rapidly diminished—a misfortune, however, that was probably reckoned among his better accidents by Owen Warland, who was becoming more and more (50) absorbed in a secret occupation which drew all his science and manual dexterity into itself, and likewise gave full employment to the characteristic tendencies of his genius.

1. The main purpose of the first paragraph is—
   A) to characterize Owen as an unconventional genius
   B) to explain how Owen came to be apprenticed at the watch shop
   C) to recall a significant event in Owen's life
   D) to describe Owen's most recent project

2. The narrator implies that Owen is—
  A) incompetent as a watchmaker
  B) overwhelmed by the details of life
  C) an outsider in his community
  D) a highly rational thinker

3. In line 12, *utilitarian* most nearly means—
  A) noble
  B) creative
  C) practical
  D) artistic

4. The description of Owen's response to the train in lines 13 through 16 primarily serves to—
  A) describe a significant, formative event in Owen's life
  B) illustrate Owen's interest in mechanical systems
  C) define Owen's unique definition of beauty
  D) further characterize Owen's peculiar affinity for the minute

5. Which choice provides the best evidence for the answer to the previous question?
  A) *But, at all events, this characteristic minuteness in his objects and accomplishments made the world even more incapable than it might otherwise have been of appreciating Owen Warland's genius.*
  B) *Peter Hovenden's opinion of his apprentice has already been expressed. He could make nothing of the lad.*
  C) *So long, however, as he remained under his old master's care, Owen's lack of sturdiness made it possible, by strict injunctions and sharp oversight, to restrain his creative eccentricity within bounds.*
  D) *One of his most rational projects was to connect a musical operation with the machinery of his watches, so that all the harsh dissonances of life might be rendered tuneful, and each flitting moment fall into the abyss of the past in golden drops of harmony.*

6. Which statement best characterizes the relationship between Owen Warland and Peter Hovenden?
  A) Owen is disinterested in Peter Hovenden's artistic endeavors.
  B) Owen is flattered to apprentice under such an accomplished watchmaker as Peter Hovenden.
  C) Peter Hovenden is perplexed by Owen's unique brilliance.
  D) Peter Hovenden resents Owen for the negative attention he has received from the community.

7. Which choice provides the best evidence for the answer to the previous question?

A) *But, at all events, this characteristic minuteness in his objects and accomplishments made the world even more incapable than it might otherwise have been of appreciating Owen Warland's genius.*

B) *Peter Hovenden's opinion of his apprentice has already been expressed. He could make nothing of the lad.*

C) *So long, however, as he remained under his old master's care, Owen's lack of sturdiness made it possible, by strict injunctions and sharp oversight, to restrain his creative eccentricity within bounds.*

D) *One of his most rational projects was to connect a musical operation with the machinery of his watches, so that all the harsh dissonances of life might be rendered tuneful, and each flitting moment fall into the abyss of the past in golden drops of harmony.*

8. As used in line 34, *eccentricity* most nearly means—

A) brilliance.

B) peculiarity.

C) energy.

D) fickleness.

9. According to the passage, Peter Hovenden turned his shop over to Owen Warland because—

A) Failing eyesight prevented him from continuing the work himself.

B) Owen had become an accomplished watchmaker and no longer needed Peter.

C) He did not understand Owen and no longer felt they could work together.

D) He was embarrassed by the reputation Owen had earned in the community.

10. The description of the *steady and matter-of-fact class of people* in lines 40 through 42 primarily serves to—

A) illustrate the open-mindedness of the community in which Owen lives

B) characterize Owen's community as responsible and reliable

C) distinguish between those who value time and those who do not

D) draw a contrast between Owen and the other members of the community

Questions 11 – 21 are based on the following passages, which address the topic of America's involvement in foreign affairs. Passage 1 is adapted from George Washington's farewell address, published in American newspapers in 1796 at the end of the president's third term. In his letter, Washington offers his advice on America's future involvement with foreign nations. Passage 2 is adapted from an address given by Harry S. Truman, the 33rd American president, before a joint session of Congress in 1947. In his speech, Truman urges Congress to provide assistance to countries at risk of Communist takeover.

Passage 1

The great rule of conduct for us, in regard to foreign nations, is, in extending our commercial relations, to have with them as little political connection as possible. So far as we have already formed engagements, let them be fulfilled with perfect good faith. Here let us stop.

(5)   Europe has a set of primary interests, which to us have none, or a very remote relation. Hence she must be engaged in frequent controversies, the causes of which are essentially foreign to our concerns. Hence, therefore, it must be unwise in us to implicate ourselves, by artificial ties, in the ordinary vicissitudes of her politics, or the ordinary combinations and collisions of her friendships or enmities.

(10)   Our detached and distant situation invites and enables us to pursue a different course. If we remain one people, under an efficient government, the period is not far off, when we may defy material injury from external annoyance; when we may take such an attitude as will cause the neutrality, we may at any time resolve upon, to be scrupulously respected; when belligerent nations, under the impossibility of making
(15) acquisitions upon us, will not lightly hazard the giving us provocation; when we may choose peace or war, as our interest, guided by justice, shall counsel.

Why forego the advantages of so peculiar a situation? Why quit our own to stand upon foreign ground? Why, by interweaving our destiny with that of any part of Europe, entangle our peace and prosperity in the toils of European ambition, rivalship, interest,
(20) humor, or caprice?

It is our true policy to steer clear of permanent alliances with any portion of the foreign world; so far, I mean, as we are now at liberty to do it; for let me not be understood as capable of patronizing infidelity to existing engagements. I hold the maxim no less applicable to public than to private affairs, that honesty is always the best policy. I
(25) repeat it, therefore, let those engagements be observed in their genuine sense. But, in my opinion, it is unnecessary and would be unwise to extend them.

Passage 2

One of the primary objectives of the foreign policy of the United States is the creation of conditions in which we and other nations will be able to work out a way of life free from coercion. This was a fundamental issue in the war with Germany and Japan. Our
(30) victory was won over countries which sought to impose their will, and their way of life, upon other nations.

To ensure the peaceful development of nations, free from coercion, the United States has taken a leading part in establishing the United Nations. The United Nations is designed to make possible lasting freedom and independence for all its members.
(35) We shall not realize our objectives, however, unless we are willing to help free peoples

to maintain their free institutions and their national integrity against aggressive movements that seek to impose upon them totalitarian regimes. This is no more than a frank recognition that totalitarian regimes imposed on free peoples, by direct or indirect aggression, undermine the foundations of international peace and hence the (40) security of the United States.

The peoples of a number of countries of the world have recently had totalitarian regimes forced upon them against their will. The Government of the United States has made frequent protests against coercion and intimidation, in violation of the Yalta agreement, in Poland, Romania, and Bulgaria. I must also state that in a number of (45) other countries there have been similar developments.

At the present moment in world history nearly every nation must choose between alternative ways of life. The choice is too often not a free one.

One way of life is based upon the will of the majority, and is distinguished by free institutions, representative government, free elections, guarantees of individual liberty, (50) freedom of speech and religion, and freedom from political oppression.

The second way of life is based upon the will of a minority forcibly imposed upon the majority. It relies upon terror and oppression, a controlled press and radio, fixed elections, and the suppression of personal freedoms.

I believe that it must be the policy of the United States to support free peoples who (55) are resisting attempted subjugation by armed minorities or by outside pressures.

I believe that we must assist free peoples to work out their own destinies in their own way.

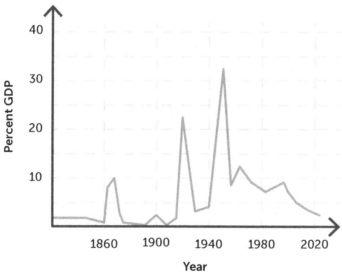

11. As used in line 8, *vicissitudes* most nearly means—

    A) fluctuations

    B) ideals

    C) mutations

    D) stagnation

12. Washington's central argument in Passage 1 is that—

   A) America should back out of the alliances it has made with other countries.

   B) America should increase its involvement with foreign nations.

   C) America should attempt to intervene in European conflicts whenever international safety is a concern.

   D) America should avoid foreign entanglements whenever it is able to do so.

13. Which choice provides the best evidence for the answer to the previous question?

   A) *It is our true policy to steer clear of permanent alliances with any portion of the foreign world; so far, I mean, as we are now at liberty to do it...*

   B) *So far as we have already formed engagements, let them be fulfilled with perfect good faith.*

   C) *Europe has a set of primary interests, which to us have none, or a very remote relation.*

   D) *If we remain one people, under an efficient government, the period is not far off, when we may defy material injury from external annoyance...*

14. Washington most likely employs a series of questions in the fourth paragraph in order to—

   A) challenge the reader to consider his own entanglements with others

   B) question the assumption that neutrality is the best course of action

   C) emphasize the absurdity of giving up a position of safe, passive neutrality

   D) minimize the impact of his opponent's counterargument

15. As used in line 43, *coercion* most nearly means—

   A) intimidation

   B) brutality

   C) cruelty

   D) authority

16. Which choice provides the best evidence for the answer to the previous question?

   A) *This was a fundamental issue in the war with Germany and Japan.*

   B) *The United Nations is designed to make possible lasting freedom and independence for all its members.*

   C) *We shall not realize our objectives, however, unless we are willing to help free peoples to maintain their free institutions and their national integrity against aggressive movements that seek to impose upon them totalitarian regimes.*

   D) *At the present moment in world history nearly every nation must choose between alternative ways of life.*

17. In Passage 2, President Truman most likely references *the war with Germany and Japan* in order to—

    A) remind Americans of the nation's stance on foreign intervention

    B) reassure Americans that they can win another war

    C) suggest a comparison between the current situation and the one that led to the war

    D) distinguish between the current situation and the one that led to America's intervention in the war

18. In lines 39 through 44, Truman most likely contrasts two ways of life in order to _____

    A) illustrate some of the benefits of a democratic government

    B) challenge the tyrannical leaders of oppressed nations to reconsider their approach to government

    C) describe the reasons that America might consider intervening in a foreign nation

    D) suggest that free people have a responsibility to fight on behalf of those who are not free

19. Which statement best describes the relationship between the passages?

    A) The two presidents take similar perspectives on foreign intervention.

    B) The two presidents take opposing perspectives on foreign intervention.

    C) The two presidents agree on most items related to foreign intervention but disagree on some key points.

    D) The two presidents agree on a few items related to foreign intervention but disagree of most key points.

20. President Truman (Passage 2) would most likely respond to Washington's claim in lines 6 through 14 by asserting that—

    A) *Our victory [in the war with Germany and Japan] was won over countries which sought to impose their will, and their way of life, upon other nations.*

    B) *To ensure the peaceful development of nations, free from coercion, the United States has taken a leading part in establishing the United Nations.*

    C) *...totalitarian regimes imposed on free peoples, by direct or indirect aggression, undermine the foundations of international peace and hence the security of the United States.*

    D) *The peoples of a number of countries of the world have recently had totalitarian regimes forced upon them against their will.*

21. Based on the passages and the graph, what conclusion can be drawn about the relationship between foreign policy and government spending in the 20th century?

    A) Government spending on national defense significantly decreased as a result of the new foreign policy approach.

    B) There was a correlation between the new foreign policy approach and increased government spending on defense.

    C) Government spending on national defense remained stagnant despite the new approach to foreign policy.

    D) There was no recognizable correlation between the new foreign policy approach and government spending on defense.

Questions 22 – 31 are based on the following passage, which provides an overview of the purpose and applications of social psychology. Information was drawn from Dr. Eliot Aronson's acclaimed book The Social Animal.

In his treatise *Politics*, Aristotle wrote, "Man is by nature a social animal; an individual who is unsocial naturally and not accidentally is either beneath our notice or more than human. Society is something in nature that precedes the individual. Anyone who either cannot lead the common life or is so self-sufficient as not to need to, and therefore does
(5) not partake of society, is either a beast or a god." For centuries, philosophers have been examining the relationship between man and his social world. It is no wonder, then, that a field of study has arisen to examine just that; the field is referred to as social psychology.

Social psychologists have been studying the effect of societal influences on human
(10) behavior for decades, and a number of fascinating findings have been the result. Together, these discoveries have shed light on one clear truth—that human behavior cannot be understood in a vacuum; that is, our daily behaviors are inextricably linked with the social context in which they occur.

Why is this important? According to social psychologist Eliot Aronson, it's
(15) important because it helps us to understand that the behaviors we witness in others may be as much a result of social influence as they are of the individual's disposition. For example, if you have ever been cut off in the middle of bad city traffic, you may have immediately assumed that the offender was inconsiderate or incompetent. While this may be true, it may be equally likely that the person is dealing with an emergency
(20) situation or that they simply did not see you. According to Aronson, this tendency to attribute behaviors, especially negative behaviors, to disposition is risky and can ultimately be detrimental to us and to the other person.

Take, for example, Philip Zimbardo's famous prison experiment, conducted at Stanford University in 1971. At the beginning of the experiment, the participants, all
(25) healthy, stable, intelligent male Stanford University students, were classified as either guards or prisoners and told they would be acting their parts in a simulated prison environment for two weeks. However, after just six days, Zimbardo had to terminate

the experiment because of the extreme behaviors he was witnessing in both groups: prisoners had become entirely submissive to and resentful of the guards, while the (30) guards had become cruel and unrelenting in their treatment of the prisoners. The otherwise healthy, well-adjusted students had experienced dramatic transformations as a result of their assigned roles. Zimbardo's conclusion? Even giving individuals temporary power over others was enough to completely alter the way they viewed and behaved toward each other; indeed, the behaviors he witnessed in each of the groups (35) were not a result of the dispositions of the participants but of the situation in which they had been placed.

Today, social psychologists study the effect of social influence on a number of different behaviors: conformity, obedience, aggression, prejudice, and even attraction and love. The insights these researchers have gained have laid the foundation for further (40) examination of human social behavior and, ultimately, for a refined approach to legal and social policy.

22. The author most likely uses the Aristotle quote in lines 1 through 5 in order to—
    A) illustrate the seriousness with which social psychology should be treated
    B) support his/her claim that curiosity about man's relationship with the social world is not a quality unique to modern thinking
    C) encourage introverts to build stronger relationships with those around them
    D) compare the social environment of beasts with the social environment of man

23. Which choice provides the best evidence for the answer to the previous question?
    A) *For centuries, philosophers have been examining the relationship between man and his social world.*
    B) *Social psychologists have been studying the effect of societal influences on human behavior for decades, and a number of fascinating findings have been the result.*
    C) *According to social psychologist Eliot Aronson, it's important because it helps us to understand that the behaviors we witness in others may be as much a result of social influence as they are of the individual's disposition.*
    D) *The insights these researchers have gained have laid the foundation for further examination of human social behavior and, ultimately, for a refined approach to legal and social policy.*

24. As used in line 12, the phrase *in a vacuum* most nearly means—
    A) without evidence of intention
    B) in conjunction with other behaviors
    C) without consideration of the individual's needs
    D) in isolation

25. The author indicates that making assumptions about people based on isolated actions is—

A) a prudent way to draw conclusions about one's social world

B) recommended when no other information is available

C) the most accurate way to assess various personality strengths

D) unwise and potentially harmful to all involved

26. In lines 24 and 25, the author most likely includes the description of the Stanford students in order to—

A) provide a contrast between their normal dispositions and the behavior they displayed during the experiment

B) engage the reader through characterization

C) illustrate the importance of quality education

D) shed light on the characteristics that made them susceptible to social influence

27. The author most likely includes the example of the Stanford Prison Experiment in order to—

A) encourage the reader to participate in social psychology studies

B) challenge the reader to question how he or she would behave in the same situation

C) illustrate the extent to which social context can influence behavior

D) undermine the reader's assumption that the quality of one's education can influence his or her behavior

28. As used in line 30, the term *unrelenting* most nearly means—

A) insistent

B) forgetful

C) remorseless

D) persistent

29. Which choice provides the best evidence for the answer to the previous question?

A) *According to Aronson, this tendency to attribute behaviors, especially negative behaviors, to disposition is risky and can ultimately be detrimental to us and to the other person.*

B) *At the beginning of the experiment, the participants, all healthy, stable, intelligent male Stanford University students, were classified as either guards or prisoners and told they would be acting their parts in a simulated prison environment for two weeks.*

C) *Even giving individuals temporary power over others was enough to completely alter the way they viewed and behaved toward each other...*

D) *Today, social psychologists study the effect of social influence on a number of different behaviors: conformity, obedience, aggression, prejudice, and even attraction and love.*

30. The author most likely includes *attraction and love* in the list in lines 38 and 39 in order to—

    A) suggest that individuals who are struggling with relationship issues should contact a social psychologist

    B) discount the assumption that social psychologists are only interested in negative human behaviors

    C) illustrate the diversity of topics that social psychologists study

    D) dispel any doubts about the qualifications of social psychologists to study human behavior

31. The author most likely includes the statement in lines 40 and 41 about legal and social policy in order to—

    A) mention one possible application for the findings of social psychologists.

    B) advocate for prison reform.

    C) criticize the work of social psychologists.

    D) dispel doubts regarding the reliability of the research of social psychologists.

Questions 32 – 41 are based on the following passage, which is adapted from an article entitled "NASA Finds Good News on Forests and Carbon Dioxide," published online by the National Aeronautics and Space Administration in December 2014.

A new NASA-led study shows that tropical forests may be absorbing far more carbon dioxide than many scientists thought, in response to rising atmospheric levels of the greenhouse gas. The study estimates that tropical forests absorb 1.4 billion metric tons of carbon dioxide out of a total global absorption of 2.5 billion—more than is absorbed
(5) by forests in Canada, Siberia and other northern regions, called boreal forests.

"This is good news, because uptake in boreal forests is already slowing, while tropical forests may continue to take up carbon for many years," said David Schimel of NASA's Jet Propulsion Laboratory, Pasadena, California. Schimel is lead author of a paper on the new research, appearing online today in the *Proceedings of National Academy of*
(10) *Sciences*.

Forests and other land vegetation currently remove up to 30 percent of human carbon dioxide emissions from the atmosphere during photosynthesis. If the rate of absorption were to slow down, the rate of global warming would speed up in return.

The new study is the first to devise a way to make apples-to-apples comparisons
(15) of carbon dioxide estimates from many sources at different scales: computer models of ecosystem processes, atmospheric models run backward in time to deduce the sources of today's concentrations (called inverse models), satellite images, data from experimental forest plots and more. The researchers reconciled all types of analyses and assessed the accuracy of the results based on how well they reproduced independent, ground-based
(20) measurements. They obtained their new estimate of the tropical carbon absorption from the models they determined to be the most trusted and verified.

"Until our analysis, no one had successfully completed a global reconciliation of information about carbon dioxide effects from the atmospheric, forestry and modeling communities," said co-author Joshua Fisher of JPL. "It is incredible that all these
(25) different types of independent data sources start to converge on an answer."

The question of which type of forest is the bigger carbon absorber "is not just an accounting curiosity," said co-author Britton Stephens of the National Center for Atmospheric Research, Boulder, Colorado. "It has big implications for our understanding of whether global terrestrial ecosystems might continue to offset our carbon dioxide
(30) emissions or might begin to exacerbate climate change."

As human-caused emissions add more carbon dioxide to the atmosphere, forests worldwide are using it to grow faster, reducing the amount that stays airborne. This effect is called carbon fertilization. "All else being equal, the effect is stronger at higher temperatures, meaning it will be higher in the tropics than in the boreal forests,"
(35) Schimel said.

But climate change also decreases water availability in some regions and makes Earth warmer, leading to more frequent and larger wildfires. In the tropics, humans compound the problem by burning wood during deforestation. Fires don't just stop carbon absorption by killing trees, they also spew huge amounts of carbon into the atmosphere as the
(40) wood burns.

For about 25 years, most computer climate models have been showing that mid-latitude forests in the Northern Hemisphere absorb more carbon than tropical forests. That result was initially based on the then-current understanding of global air flows and limited data suggesting that deforestation was causing tropical forests to release
(45) more carbon dioxide than they were absorbing.

In the mid-2000s, Stephens used measurements of carbon dioxide made from aircraft to show that many climate models were not correctly representing flows of carbon above ground level. Models that matched the aircraft measurements better showed more carbon absorption in the tropical forests. However, there were still not
(50) enough global data sets to validate the idea of a large tropical-forest absorption. Schimel said that their new study took advantage of a great deal of work other scientists have done since Stephens' paper to pull together national and regional data of various kinds into robust, global data sets.

Schimel noted that their paper reconciles results at every scale from the pores of a
(55) single leaf, where photosynthesis takes place, to the whole Earth, as air moves carbon dioxide around the globe. "What we've had up till this paper was a theory of carbon dioxide fertilization based on phenomena at the microscopic scale and observations at the global scale that appeared to contradict those phenomena. Here, at least, is a hypothesis that provides a consistent explanation that includes both how we know
(60) photosynthesis works and what's happening at the planetary scale."

32. As it is used in line 18, the term *reconciled* most nearly means—

    A) forgave.

    B) studied.

    C) integrated.

    D) gathered.

33. Which choice provides the best evidence for the answer to the previous question?

    A) *They obtained their new estimate of the tropical carbon absorption from the models they determined to be the most trusted and verified.*

    B) *"It is incredible that all these different types of independent data sources start to converge on an answer."*

    C) *That result was initially based on the then-current understanding of global air flows and limited data suggesting that deforestation was causing tropical forests to release more carbon dioxide than they were absorbing.*

    D) *Models that matched the aircraft measurements better showed more carbon absorption in the tropical forests. However, there were still not enough global data sets to validate the idea of a large tropical-forest absorption.*

34. According to the passage, what is the relationship between photosynthesis and global warming?

    A) Photosynthesis allows carbon dioxide gas to be released into the atmosphere, exacerbating the issue of global warming.

    B) Carbon dioxide prevents trees from flourishing, thus increasing the amount of greenhouse gas and exacerbating the issue of global warming.

    C) Trees absorb carbon dioxide during photosynthesis, removing much of the carbon dioxide from the atmosphere and slowing the effects of global warming.

    D) Greenhouse gases like carbon dioxide slow the effects of global warming by prevent trees from completing the cycle of photosynthesis.

35. The passage indicates that research into carbon dioxide absorption is significant because—

    A) It challenges us to question our own opinions on global warming and climate change.

    B) It forces us to recognize that global warming poses a significant threat to our vegetation.

    C) It encourages us to consider whether forests are effective alternatives to carbon dioxide emissions.

    D) It allows us to understand the impact of the earth's forests on climate change.

36. The passage indicates that wildfires—

A) both result from and contribute to climate change

B) are the most significant contributor to climate change

C) occur when temperature and humidity are both high

D) have little to no effect on carbon dioxide emissions

37. According to the passage, increased carbon dioxide emissions may result in—

A) increased water availability.

B) smaller, less frequent wildfires.

C) faster-growing forests.

D) decreased oxygen availability.

38. A student claims that preserving the earth's forests is an essential step in slowing climate change. Which of the following statements from the passage supports this student's claim?

A) "This is good news, because uptake in boreal forests is already slowing, while tropical forests may continue to take up carbon for many years," said David Schimel of NASA's Jet Propulsion Laboratory, Pasadena, California.

B) If the rate of absorption [of carbon dioxide] were to slow down, the rate of global warming would speed up in return.

C) But climate change also decreases water availability in some regions and makes Earth warmer, leading to more frequent and larger wildfires.

D) That result was initially based on the then-current understanding of global air flows and limited data suggesting that deforestation was causing tropical forests to release more carbon dioxide than they were absorbing.

39. As used in line 53, the term *robust* most nearly means—

A) round

B) comprehensive

C) sturdy

D) prosperous

40. The author mostly likely mentions the Stephens study in lines 46 through 49 in order to—

A) criticize the work of environmental scientists before Stephens

B) demonstrate the effect that a limited data set can have on the results of an experiment

C) question the findings of Stephens and his colleagues

D) emphasize the need for thorough data sets in drawing conclusions about climate change

41. According to the final paragraph (lines 54 through 60), NASA's recent study into carbon dioxide absorption was significant because—

A) it provided insight into the absorption speeds of two different kinds of forests.

B) it offered a hypothesis on how to predict and prevent wildfires.

C) it demonstrated the power of collaborative research methods.

D) it resulted in a theory of climate change that accommodated both large and small-scale considerations.

Questions 42 – 52 are based on the following passage, which is adapted from an article entitled "NASA Contributes to First Global Review of Arctic Marine Mammals," published online by the National Aeronautics and Space Administration in April 2015. The accompanying graphic was initially published to NASA's Cryosphere Science Research Portal, alongside an article entitled "Current State of the Sea Ice Cover."

Many human communities want answers about the current status and future of Arctic marine mammals, including scientists who dedicate their lives to studying them and indigenous people whose traditional ways of subsistence are intertwined with the fate of species such as ice seals, narwhals, walruses and polar bears.

(5)   But there are many unknowns about the current status of eleven species of marine mammals who depend on Arctic sea ice to live, feed and breed, and about how their fragile habitat will evolve in a warming world.

A recently published multinational study attempted to gauge the population trends of Arctic marine mammals and changes in their habitat, identify missing scientific
(10) information, and provide recommendations for the conservation of Arctic marine mammals over the next decades.

The Arctic sea ice cover, made of frozen seawater floating on top of the Arctic Ocean and its neighboring seas, naturally grows in the fall and winter and melts during the spring and summer every year. But over the past decades, the melt season has grown
(15) longer and the average extent of Arctic sea ice has diminished, changing the game for many Arctic marine mammals—namely beluga, narwhal and bowhead whales; ringed, bearded, spotted, ribbon, harp and hooded seals; walruses; and polar bears.

"This research would not have been possible without support from NASA," said Kristin Laidre, lead author of the new study and a polar scientist with University of
(20) Washington in Seattle. "NASA backed us on research related to the biodiversity and ecology of Arctic marine mammals, as well as the development of metrics for the loss of sea ice, their habitat."

Laidre's team used the Arctic sea ice record derived from microwave measurements taken by NASA and Department of Defense satellites. This record began in late 1978, (25) is uninterrupted, and relies on NASA-developed methods for processing the microwave data.

"It's really our best global view of the Arctic sea ice," said Harry Stern, author of the paper with Laidre and a mathematician specializing in sea ice and climate at University of Washington.

(30) Stern divided the Arctic Ocean into twelve regions. Using daily sea ice concentration data from the satellite record, he calculated changes in the dates of the beginning of the melt season in spring and the start of the fall freeze-up from 1979 to 2013. He found that, in all regions but one, the melt season had grown longer (mostly by five to ten weeks, and by twenty weeks in one region).

(35) "Sea ice is critical for Arctic marine mammals because events such as feeding, giving birth, molting, and resting are closely timed with the availability of their ice platform," Laidre said. "It is especially critical for the ice-dependent species—seals and polar bears. Ice seals use the sea ice platform to give birth and nurse pups during very specific weeks of the spring, and polar bears use sea ice for feeding, starting in late winter and (40) continuing until the ice breaks up."

Pacific walrus use the floating pack ice both as a platform on which to rest between feeding bouts and as a passive transport around their habitat.

"Loss of sea ice has resulted in walrus hauling out on land in Alaska and Russia in massive numbers—these land haul outs result in trampling of their young," Laidre (45) said. "Also, now walrus must travel a longer way to reach their feeding areas, which is energetically costly."

In the case of Arctic whales, the changes in sea ice might benefit their populations, at least in the short term: the loss and earlier retreat of sea ice opens up new habitats and, in some areas of the Arctic, has also led to an increase in food production and the (50) length of their feeding season.

In the future, Stern said higher-resolution satellite microwave data might come in handy when studying the interactions of Arctic marine mammals with their icy habitat.

"For example, we know that narwhals congregate in specific areas of the Arctic in the wintertime, so maybe a higher spatial resolution in these areas might help us better (55) understand their relationship with the ice," Stern said. "But mainly, just continuing daily coverage is what's important for the long-term monitoring of habitat changes."

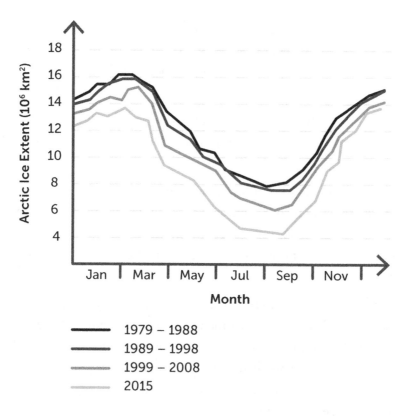

Arctic Ice Extent (10⁶ km²) vs Month

Legend:
- 1979 – 1988
- 1989 – 1998
- 1999 – 2008
- 2015

42. In the first paragraph, the author includes a detail about indigenous people of the Arctic in order to—

A) provide readers with a relatable story to consider as they read the article

B) emphasize the importance of protecting the habitats of Arctic marine mammals

C) challenge readers to make Arctic preservation efforts their top priority

D) illustrate a contrast between the indigenous people and the scientists mentioned in the first part of the sentence

43. In lines 12 through 17, the author indicates that while fluctuation in sea ice extent is expected throughout the year—

A) variability from year to year is a recent phenomenon.

B) the fluctuation is usually minute.

C) daily changes in sea ice extent are becoming more typical.

D) changes in the populations of Arctic mammals are not.

44. The author most likely includes the list of Arctic marine mammals in lines 16 through 17 in order to—

A) illustrate a discrepancy between the number of Arctic species and the number of species that depend on sea ice for survival

B) challenge the assertion that the recession of sea ice is significant

C) articulate a general truth about life in the Arctic

D) highlight the number of species that depend on sea ice for their survival

45. The passage indicates that when it comes to research about sea ice and the animals who rely on it—

A) Scientists know everything they need to know.

B) Data collection is rarely a simple process.

C) Very few answers currently exist.

D) Vigilant observation is an essential tool in gaining insight.

46. As used in line 7, the term *fragile* most nearly means—

A) brittle

B) flimsy

C) breakable

D) unstable

47. Which choice provides the best evidence for the answer to the previous question?

A) *Using daily sea ice concentration data from the satellite record, he calculated changes in the dates of the beginning of the melt season in spring and the start of the fall freeze-up from 1979 to 2013.*

B) *"Sea ice is critical for Arctic marine mammals because events such as feeding, giving birth, molting, and resting are closely timed with the availability of their ice platform[.]"*

C) *The Arctic sea ice cover, made of frozen seawater floating on top of the Arctic Ocean and its neighboring seas, naturally grows in the fall and winter and melts during the spring and summer every year.*

D) *But over the past decades, the melt season has grown longer and the average extent of Arctic sea ice has diminished, changing the game for many Arctic marine mammals...*

48. The passage indicates that in a little over three decades, the length of the melt seasons in most regions of the Arctic—

A) decreased by more than two months

B) increased by more than two months

C) decreased by more than a month

D) increased by more than a month

49. In lines 32 through 46, the author indicates that—

A) Most, but not all, animals struggle when the availability of sea ice decreases.

B) Many animals will continue to thrive despite the change in climate.

C) All Arctic mammals use sea ice for the same reason.

D) All Arctic mammals struggle when the availability of sea ice decreases.

50. As it is used in line 48, the term *retreat* most nearly means—

A) surrender

B) refuge

C) recession

D) departure

51. Which choice provides the best evidence for the answer to the previous question?

A) *But there are many unknowns about the current status of 11 species of marine mammals who depend on Arctic sea ice to live, feed and breed, and about how their fragile habitat will evolve in a warming world.*

B) *Using daily sea ice concentration data from the satellite record, he calculated changes in the dates of the beginning of the melt season in spring and the start of the fall freeze-up from 1979 to 2013.*

C) *In the future, Stern said higher-resolution satellite microwave data might come in handy when studying the interactions of Arctic marine mammals with their icy habitat.*

D) *"But mainly, just continuing daily coverage is what's important for the long-term monitoring of habitat changes."*

52. Which claim about Arctic ice extent is supported by the graph?

A) Arctic ice extent has remained steady over the last three decades.

B) Patterns of formation and recession are largely unpredictable.

C) Arctic ice extent during late summer is significantly lower today than it was in 1979.

D) Sea ice extent during winter was significantly lower in 1979 than it is today.

Writing and Language

In the following passages, there are numbered and underlined words and phrases that correspond with the questions. You are to choose the answer that best completes the statement grammatically, stylistically, and/or logically. If you think the original version is best, select "NO CHANGE."

AEROSPACE ENGINEERING

In the 21st century, the growing population and the public interest in space exploration will undoubtedly call for increased investment in air and space travel. (1)Therefore, individuals who excel at maths and sciences and are interested in a full-time career with high salaries and job security ought to consider a career in aerospace engineering.

1. Which of the following choices most effectively frames the main argument of the passage?
   A) NO CHANGE
   B) As such, individuals who enjoy a good challenge ought to consider a career in aerospace engineering.
   C) Accordingly, individuals who want to start a career should consider pursuing aerospace engineering.
   D) Consequently, individuals who like space should consider starting a career in aerospace engineering.

Aerospace engineers typically get to choose from one of two (2)concentrations such as aeronautical engineering or astronautical engineering—and as a result are able to focus their efforts in the field that most interests them. Aeronautical engineers work on designing and constructing aircraft for travel within the earth's

2. A) NO CHANGE
   B) concentrations, aeronautical engineering
   C) concentrations—aeronautical engineering
   D) concentrations. Aeronautical engineering

(3)atmosphere, astronautical engineers, on the other hand, build spacecraft for use both inside and outside of earth's atmosphere. Though the two specialties have their own

3. A) NO CHANGE
    B) atmosphere and astronautical engineers
    C) atmosphere, however, astronautical engineers
    D) atmosphere; astronautical engineers

(4)unique challenges and demands, both require a strong grasp of physics and higher-level mathematics, so individuals who excel at logical reasoning are well-suited for these fields.

4. A) NO CHANGE
    B) challenging demands
    C) challenges
    D) demand that are challenging

Aerospace engineers typically work full time schedules and, when in leadership positions, may work as much as fifty or sixty hours per week. The bulk of those hours occurs in an office setting, where these engineers use advanced software programs to design models and run simulations. Most of these individuals work for firms that are contracted out to the federal government; they may contribute to the design and construction of aircraft, missiles, or systems for national defense. As a result, many aerospace engineering jobs require advanced security clearance. Citizenship in the U.S. may even be a requirement for many positions.

Like other kinds of engineers, aerospace engineers must have a bachelor's degree in their field. While in school, (5)they studied advanced calculus, trigonometry, general engineering, and physics (including propulsion, mechanics, structures, and aerodynamics). As a result, the degree is typically more rigorous than degrees in other areas of engineering.

5. A) NO CHANGE
    B) they must study
    C) they would study
    D) they will study

(6)However, aerospace engineers usually see a much bigger payoff in terms of salary than do other engineers: <u>the median salary for aerospace engineers is quite a bit larger than the median salary for other engineering professions.</u>

(7)

6. Which of the following completes this sentence with accurate information from the graph at the conclusion of the passage?

   A) NO CHANGE

   B) the median salary for aerospace engineers is almost twenty thousand dollars more than the median salary for other engineering professions.

   C) the median salary for aerospace engineers is almost fifty thousand dollars more than the median salary for other engineering professions.

   D) the median salary for aerospace engineers is about the same as the median salary for other engineering professions.

7. For the sake of logical coherence, the preceding sentence should be placed—

   A) where it is now

   B) at the beginning of the paragraph

   C) after the first sentence

   D) after the second sentence

(8) In 2012, the United States Bureau of Labor Statistics projected that the profession of aerospace engineering would expand by seven percent before 2022, creating over six thousand new jobs over the next decade. Further, opportunities for advancement

8. Which of the following provides the most effective transition from the previous paragraph to this one?
   A) The Bureau of Labor Statistics researches various professions to gather information about the changing job market.
   B) The field of aerospace engineering is not shrinking.
   C) In addition to earning a high salary, aerospace engineers can expect a high level of job security.
   D) Aerospace engineering is clearly a great option for those entering the workforce.

(9) is plentiful. Aerospace engineers

9. A) NO CHANGE
   B) are
   C) were
   D) was

(10) which excel in their field can work their way toward careers as technical specialists, supervisors, or even engineering or program

10. A) NO CHANGE
    B) whom
    C) that
    D) who

managers. (11)

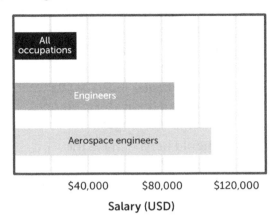

Salary (USD)

YOUNG ABRAHAM

A young Abraham Lincoln awoke with a (12)jolt, excited to pick up where he had left off with his reading. He had chores to complete in the morning, of course, but he loved those days when he could fit in a couple hours of studying before he had to begin with his work.

11. At this point, the writer is considering adding the following sentence:

By taking advantage of apprenticeships or advanced educational opportunities, aerospace engineers can increase their chances of advancement in their field.

Should the writer make this addition?

A) Yes, because it emphasizes the possibility of career advancement for aerospace engineers and provides some insight into how that advancement is earned.

B) Yes, because it provides important information about additional requirements that an entry-level aerospace engineer might have to complete.

C) No, because advancement is most likely not a significant factor for graduates entering the field of aerospace engineering.

D) No, because individuals who are interested in aerospace engineering should not be worried about advancement so early in their career.

12. A) NO CHANGE

B) jolt, being excited

C) jolt and excited

D) jolt; excited

<u>(13)</u>

13. At this point, the writer is considering adding the following sentence:

He was especially looking forward to the quiet time on this particular morning: he was reading a book about his hero, George Washington.

Should he/she make this addition?

A) Yes, because it gives the reader insight into who Lincoln admired as a young boy.

B) Yes, because it provides information about the events that are about to unfold.

C) No, because it distracts the reader from the main point of the paragraph.

D) No, because the detail is irrelevant to the narrative.

Young Abe <u>(14)rolled over, stretches his arms, and reaches toward the wall,</u> where he had lodged his book between two of the logs that constructed his family's cabin. *Oh no*, he thought as he felt the book's binding.

14. A) NO CHANGE

B) rolls over, stretching his arms, and reaches toward the wall,

C) rolling over, stretching his arms, and reaching toward the wall,

D) rolled over, stretched his arms, and reached toward the wall,

It was noticeably <u>(15)sopping</u> and had been warped

15. A) NO CHANGE

B) drenched

C) damp

D) soaking

by the moisture: (16)evidently it had rained most of the previous night. He pulled the book from its slot in the wall and set it down in front of him.

Oh no, he repeated to himself. Young Abe was a dedicated and diligent reader, but because of his family's financial situation, he could not afford to buy his own books. He read only when he could find a book to borrow, (17)which unfortunately was not often.

(18)This book, *The Life of Washington*, was one of his favorites. He had borrowed this wonderful book from his teacher, Andrew Crawford, by whom he had been instructed in manners and composition. He knew he had to tell Crawford the truth about his book, but he was petrified by the thought of admitting his mistake. Still, Abe decided, it was the right thing to do. He attempted to dry the book's pages as best he could and set it aside.

16. Which choice provides the most relevant detail at this point in the narrative?
    A) NO CHANGE
    B) Evidently the pages were thinner than Lincoln had realized.
    C) Evidently the book was a popular one.
    D) Evidently the book had not budged at all while young Lincoln slept.

17. Which choice most effectively illustrates the young Abe Lincoln's commitment to learning?
    A) NO CHANGE
    B) and he had a fine reputation for being cautious with the books he borrowed
    C) so he had only read a handful of books
    D) sometimes walking miles to retrieve it

18. The writer is considering deleting the underlined sentence. Should he/she make this deletion?
    A) Yes, because it gives away the ending of the narrative.
    B) Yes, because it attributes undue importance to the book itself.
    C) No, because it provides important insight into why the incident was so disappointing.
    D) No, because it sheds light on who Lincoln was as a child.

(19)

Later that afternoon, young Abe stepped out into the crisp autumn air to make the journey to the Crawford home, (20)wear he would have to deliver the news about the ruined book. He took a deep breath and began to walk.

Before long, he found himself at the door of the Crawford home, talking to the man himself. "So you see," Young Abe stammered, "I intended to take good care of your book, but it seems I made an error in judgment. I hope you will allow me to repay you for my blunder." Crawford and Abe both knew that (21)he had no money and that the only way he could pay was through work.

"Give me three (22)day's work on the harvest," said Crawford, "and the manuscript is yours."

Young Abraham Lincoln was jubilant. Of course the three days of harvesting corn in the Crawford's field would not be ideal, but at the end of it, he would be the proud owner of a shabby—but readable—copy of *The Life of Washington*.

19. For the sake of logic and coherence, the preceding paragraph should be placed—
   A) where it is now
   B) at the beginning of the narrative
   C) after the first paragraph
   D) after the second paragraph

20. A) NO CHANGE
    B) where
    C) were
    D) whir

21. A) NO CHANGE
    B) they
    C) the boy
    D) him

22. A) NO CHANGE
    B) days
    C) daze
    D) days'

GLOBAL FOOD PRODUCTION

Environmental concerns have been at the center of ongoing debate in the 21st century: we are going green in both our homes and our offices, and discourse around renewable energy sources, responsible recycling, and threatening pollution (23)are commonplace. Still, according to acclaimed environmental scientist Dr. Jonathon Foley, for all of our concern about the environment, we often

(24)overlook one of the most significant threats to our planet: global food production.

(25)Though we must make food in order to survive as a species, we do not have to do it irresponsibly.

The threat of global food production is manifest in many forms. Greenhouse gases such as methane, nitrous oxide, and carbon dioxide are released in larger amounts by farming and agricultural practices (26) than all the world's transportation vehicles combined. Additionally, the world's limited water supply is both depleted and polluted by farming and agricultural techniques.

23. **A)** NO CHANGE
B) were
C) is
D) was

24. **A)** NO CHANGE
B) oversee
C) disregard
D) overview

25. **A)** NO CHANGE
B) Incidentally
C) Until
D) When

26. **A)** NO CHANGE
B) than are all the
C) than by all the
D) than do all the

(27)The further clearing of land for crops poses a threat to indigenous wildlife in some areas and has, in some cases substantially, contributed to species extinction.

27.
A) NO CHANGE

B) Further, the clearing of land for crops in some areas poses a threat to indigenous wildlife and has contributed, in some cases substantially, to species extinction.

C) In some cases substantially, the clearing of land for crops poses a threat in some areas to indigenous wildlife and has contributed to species extinction.

D) In some areas, the clearing of further land for crops has contributed, in some cases substantially, to species extinction and poses a threat to indigenous wildlife.

(28)

28. At this point, the writer is considering adding the following sentence:

Altogether, the threat that is posed to our planet by our own food production practices is one that we can no longer afford to ignore.

Should the writer make this addition?

A) Yes, because it ties together the author's ideas about sustainability and affordability.

B) Yes, because it provides a brief summary of the previous paragraph and an effective transition into the next paragraph.

C) No, because it distracts the reader from the main point of the paragraph.

D) No, because the tone does not align with the author's purpose.

Fortunately, researchers like Dr. Foley have committed (29)his career to finding solutions to these challenges. In fact, Foley has refined a clear, five-step system that he believes will lead to significant positive change.

First, says Foley, we must halt agricultural expansion. Globally, (30)land devoted to food productions accounts for an area as large as South America and Africa combined. Moving forward, we must commit to preserving natural habits where they currently exist. Second, we must seek to expand production on the lands we have already committed to farming.

(31)Especially in those areas where crop yields are low, new technologies have the potential to significantly increase yields and improve efficiency. Third, we must learn to make better use of our precious, non-renewable resources like water. By borrowing techniques from commercial and organic farming,

29. **A)** NO CHANGE
    B) there careers
    C) their careers
    D) they're careers

30. **A)** NO CHANGE
    B) land devoted to food production account
    C) lands devoted to food production account
    D) lands devoted to food production accounts

31. **A)** NO CHANGE
    B) Significantly, in those areas where crop yields are low, new technologies especially have the potential to increase yields and improve efficiency.
    C) New technologies have the potential where crop yields are significantly low to improve efficiency and increase yields.
    D) Where crop yields are significantly low, new technologies especially have the potential to improve efficiency and increase yields.

(32)farmers around the world can begin to make more conscious choices about efficient water use and protect water sources from contamination.

Fourth, we must reconsider the structures of our diets. Today, more than thirty-five percent of the world's crops are used to feed livestock, but only a small percent of the calories consumed by these animals make it into human diets. By designing diets that are less reliant on meat proteins, we can return some of those crop yields, and calories, to the global food bank. Finally, we must work to minimize food waste worldwide by buying and using food products more consciously.

32. A) NO CHANGE

B) farmers around the world can begin to make more conscious choices about using water efficiently and protecting water sources from contamination.

C) farmers around the world can begin to make more conscious choices about efficient water use and protecting water sources from contamination.

D) farmers around the world can begin to make more conscious choices about efficient water use and protect water sources from contamination.

<u>(33)</u>

33. At this point the writer wants to add a concluding statement. Which of the following provides a conclusion that is appropriate to both the tone and purpose of the passage?

A) These changes will be especially challenging in developed countries, where food production costs are high and meals are easier to come by.

B) By following these simple steps in countries all around the globe, we can begin to make positive changes that will feed our population while protecting our environment.

C) While these changes will no doubt be challenging for us as a population, we can definitely make them work for us.

D) By taking these simple steps in countries around the globe, we can ensure that there will be enough food to feed the entire human population.

Go On

THE ORIGINS OF HUMANITY?

(34)Charles Darwin wrote *The Origin of Species* over one hundred years ago, in 1859. However, musings on the beginnings of human existence are by no means unique to our modern

34. Which of the following most effectively introduces the topic of the article by relating to the modern reader?

   A) NO CHANGE

   B) There is currently no way for us to know where our species came from or how we were when we first appeared.

   C) Philosophers have, for centuries, pondered the meaning and origins of human life on Earth.

   D) In today's technologically advanced world, scientists are spending more time than ever asking questions about the origins of our planet and our species.

mind. (35) Indeed, creation myths are numerous and varied. Despite their differences, however, the universal theme of

35. At this point, the writer wants to add additional support for the paragraph's main point. Which choice most effectively accomplishes this goal?

   A) Even centuries ago, the earliest human civilizations sought to understand where they came from.

   B) In fact, modern sciences also seek to understand how our universe itself came to be.

   C) Scientists have never been clearer about where the human species came from.

   D) Still, it is important to be content with one's own understanding, so as not to become dependent on others for one's ideas.

(36)this story highlights the instinctive desire that exists in all cultures to understand how our species came to be.

Some early civilizations subscribed to beliefs about man's evolution from nature. According to Sanchuniathon, an ancient Phoenician mythographer, all things on Earth, including humanity, evolved from the winds themselves. The winds swirled around each other to produce Desire, which eventually took form as a slimy substance called Mot. From Mot (37)was born simple creatures that eventually evolved into conscious human beings.

(38)However, the early peoples of southern California believed humanity evolved from animals—coyotes in particular. According to the legend, coyotes began their evolution when they started sitting up to bury their dead. (39)Over time, their tails were worn down, their paws lengthened, and their snouts shortened into human noses.

36. **A)** NO CHANGE
    B) these stories highlights
    C) this story highlight
    D) these stories highlight

37. **A)** NO CHANGE
    B) were born simple creatures
    C) was born a simple creature
    D) were born a simple creature

38. **A)** NO CHANGE
    B) Consequently,
    C) Regardless,
    D) In a similar manner,

39. At this point, the writer is considering deleting the underlined sentence. Should he/she make this deletion?
    A) Yes, because it distracts the reader from the main point of the paragraph.
    B) Yes, because the reader already understands that humans evolved from coyotes.
    C) No, because it provides further detail about how the early tribes of southern California believed humans evolved from coyotes.
    D) No, because it provides a humorous detail that helps readers to relate to the people who believed this myth.

The early Borneo people had their own myth about (40)humanities beginning: they believed that humanity was born out of a

rock, which one day opened (41)her mouth to let the first humans walk out. Those humans, through their hard work and sacrifices, grew the rest of the earth and its inhabitants.

(42)Still, not all ancient peoples believed humans evolved from nature. Some mythologies included stories of humanity's creation by deities. According to Mesopotamian myth, for example, Marduk, the fierce god of the sun, created humanity out of the body of another god, Tiamat,

(43)who he had defeated in an epic battle.

According to the mythology of the Hopi Indians, Tawa, the Sun Spirit, was responsible for the creation of humanity. Their legend stated that Tawa created the first world, which to his disappointment was inhabited only by insects that could not understand the meaning of life. To elevate his creation, he formed a second world and forced the insects to climb to it. Over the course of this challenging journey, they

40. A) NO CHANGE
    B) humanity's
    C) humanity
    D) the human

41. A) NO CHANGE
    B) his
    C) it's
    D) its

42. Which choice provides the most effective, appropriate transition from the previous paragraph to this one?
    A) NO CHANGE
    B) Regardless of their location, many primitive populations used these kinds of myths to make sense of their world.
    C) If humanity's evolution from nature was not crazy enough, other cultures believed even crazier myths.
    D) In spite of information to the contrary, myths about humanity's evolution from nature were not especially popular.

43. A) NO CHANGE
    B) who it had defeated
    C) whom he had defeated
    D) whom it had defeated

evolved into more complex creatures and eventually into humans.

Other civilizations believed humanity was (44)neither a descendant of the earth or a creation of the gods: these peoples believed that humanity descended directly from the gods themselves. According to the Hindu creation myth, for example, the deity Purusha, who was both man and woman, was split in half. The two halves of the deity united and continued to reunite in different forms until all of the creatures on Earth had been created.

44. **A)** NO CHANGE

   B) neither a descendant of the earth nor a creation of the gods

   C) either a descendant of the earth or a creation of the gods

   D) both a descendant of the earth and a creation of the gods

Mathematics

For questions 1 – 15, work the problem and choose the most correct answer. For questions 16 – 20, work the problem and write in the correct answer in the space provided.

FORMULA CHART

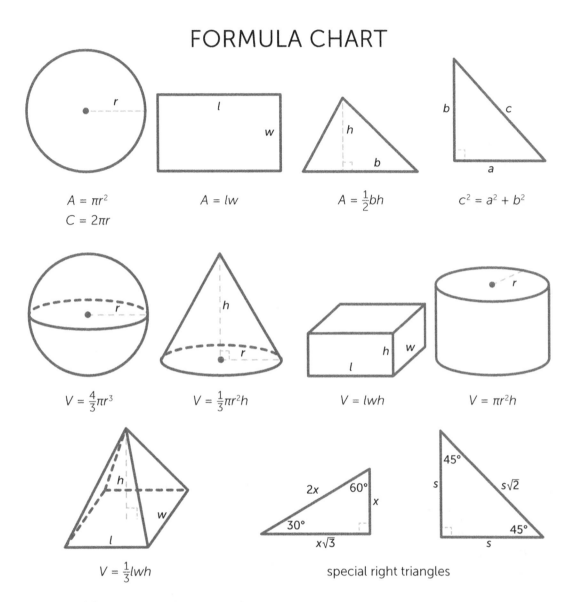

$A = \pi r^2$

$C = 2\pi r$

$A = lw$

$A = \frac{1}{2}bh$

$c^2 = a^2 + b^2$

$V = \frac{4}{3}\pi r^3$

$V = \frac{1}{3}\pi r^2 h$

$V = lwh$

$V = \pi r^2 h$

$V = \frac{1}{3}lwh$

special right triangles

▶ The number of degrees of arc in a circle is 360.

▶ The number of radians of arc in a circle is 2π.

▶ The sum of the measures in degrees of the angles of a triangle is 180.

NO CALCULATOR
Multiple-Choice

1. What is the axis of symmetry for the given parabola?

   $y = -2(x + 3)^2 + 5$

   A) $y = 3$

   B) $x = -3$

   C) $y = -3$

   D) $x = 3$

2. Which of the following is equivalent to $z^3(z + 2)^2 - 4z^3 + 2$?

   A) 2

   B) $z^5 + 4z^4 + 4z^3 + 2$

   C) $z^6 + 4z^3 + 2$

   D) $z^5 + 4z^4 + 2$

3. Which of the following is an equation of the line that passes through the points $(4,-3)$ and $(-2,9)$ in the xy-plane?

   A) $y = -2x + 5$

   B) $y = -\frac{1}{2}x - 1$

   C) $y = \frac{1}{2}x - 5$

   D) $y = 2x - 11$

4. What is the domain of the inequality $\left|\frac{x}{8}\right| \geq 1$?

   A) $(-\infty,\infty)$

   B) $[8,\infty)$

   C) $(-\infty,-8]$

   D) $(-\infty,-8] \cup [8,\infty)$

5. What is the greatest number of complex roots a 17th degree polynomial can have?

   A) 8

   B) 17

   C) 16

   D) $16i$

6. In the xy-plane, the line given by which of the following equations is parallel to the line $3x + 2y = 10$?

   A) $y = -3x + 2$

   B) $y = -\frac{3}{2}x + 5$

   C) $y = \frac{1}{3}x + 5$

   D) $y = \frac{2}{3}x - 10$

7. Which of the following represents a linear equation?

   A) $\sqrt[3]{y} = x$

   B) $\sqrt[3]{x} = y$

   C) $\sqrt[3]{y} = x^2$

   D) $y = \sqrt[3]{x^3}$

8. Justin has a summer lawn care business and earns $40 for each lawn he mows. He also pays $35 per week in business expenses. Which of the following expressions represents Justin's profit after x weeks if he mows m number of lawns?

   A) $40m - 35x$

   B) $40m + 35x$

   C) $35x(40 + m)$

   D) $35(40m + x)$

9. What are the real zero(s) of the following polynomial?

   $2n^2 + 2n - 12 = 0$

   A) (2)

   B) $(-3,2)$

   C) $(2,4)$

   D) There are no real zeros of n.

10. Which graph shows the solution to $y = 2x + 1$?

A)

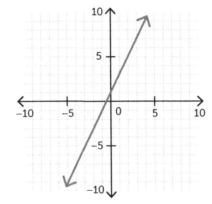

B)

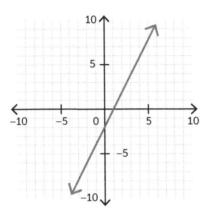

C)

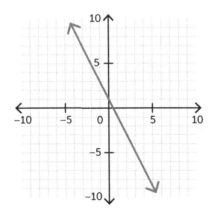

D)

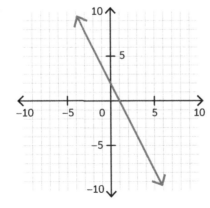

11. A cube with volume 27 cubic meters is inscribed within a sphere such that all of the cube's vertices touch the sphere. What is the length of the sphere's radius?

A) 2.6 meters

B) 3 meters

C) 5.2 meters

D) 9 meters

12. Find the value of x in the triangle below.

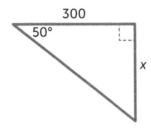

A) 300(sin 50°)

B) 300(cos 50°)

C) 300(tan 50°)

D) 300(csc 50°)

13. What is the domain of the piece-wise function shown in the graph?

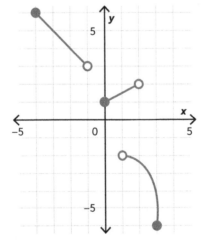

A) D: $[-4,-1) \cup [0,3]$

B) D: $(-4,3)$

C) D: $[-4,1] \cup (0,3)$

D) D: $(-4,-1) \cup [0,1) \cup [1,3]$

14. Which of the following defines y as a function of x?

I. $y^2 + x = 3$

II.

x	y
0	4
1	5
2	8
3	13
4	20

III.

$y = \sin(\theta)$

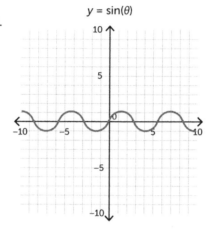

A) II only

B) I and II only

C) II and III only

D) I, II, III only

15. Which of the following is the vertical asymptote of the given function?

$$f(x) = \frac{x+4}{-2x-6}$$

A) $y = \frac{1}{2}$

B) $y = -2$

C) $x = 3$

D) $x = -3$

16. What is the slope of the graph below?

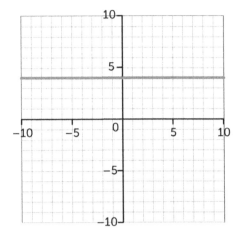

----

17. Solve the equation: $\sqrt{2x - 5} + 4 = x$

----

18. Given the diagram, if $XZ = 100$, $WZ = 80$, and $XU = 70$, then $WY = ?$

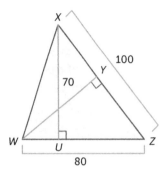

----

19. What is the y-intercept of the given equation?

$7y - 42x + 7 = 0$

----

20. If $16^{x + 10} = 83x$, what is the value of x?

CALCULATOR
Multiple Choice

For questions 1 – 30, work the problem and choose the most correct answer. For questions 31 – 38, work the problem and write in the correct answer in the space provided.

1. If a student answers 42 out of 48 questions correctly on a quiz, what percentage of questions did she answer correctly?

A) 82.5%

B) 85%

C) 87.5%

D) 90%

2. The population of a town was 7,250 in 2014 and 7,375 in 2015. What was the percent increase from 2014 to 2015 to the nearest tenth of a percent?

A) 1.5%

B) 1.6%

C) 1.7%

D) 1.8%

3. What are the roots of the equation $y = 16x^3 - 48x^2$?

A) $\left(\dfrac{3 + i\sqrt{5}}{2}, \dfrac{3 - i\sqrt{5}}{2}\right)$

B) $(0, 3, -3)$

C) $(0, 3i, -3i)$

D) $(0, 3)$

4. Bryce has 34 coins worth a total of $6.25. If all the coins are dimes or quarters, how many of each coin does he have?

A) 9 dimes and 15 quarters

B) 10 dimes and 24 quarters

C) 15 dimes and 19 quarters

D) 19 dimes and 15 quarters

5. Which of the following is a solution to the inequality $2x + y \le -10$?

A) (0,0)

B) (10,2)

C) (10,10)

D) (−10,−10)

6. An ice chest contains 24 sodas, some regular and some diet. The ratio of diet soda to regular soda is 1:3. How many regular sodas are there in the ice chest?

A) 1

B) 4

C) 18

D) 24

7. A square-based pyramid has a height of 10 cm. If the length of the side of the square is 6 cm, what is the surface area of the pyramid?

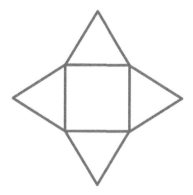

A) 36 cm

B) $3\sqrt{109}$ cm

C) 100 cm

D) 161.3 cm

8. In the circle below with center O, the minor arc ACB measures 5 feet. What is the measurement of $m\angle AOB$?

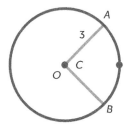

A) 90

B) 90.5

C) 95

D) 95.5

9. In the fall, 425 students pass the math benchmark. In the spring, 680 students pass the same benchmark. What is the percentage increase in passing scores from fall to spring?

A) 37.5%

B) 55%

C) 60%

D) 62.5%

10. A baby weighed 7.5 pounds at birth and gained weight at a rate of 6 ounces per month for the first six months. Which equation describes the baby's weight in ounces, y, after t months?

A) $y = 6t - 7.5$

B) $y = 6t + 120$

C) $y = 7.5t + 120$

D) $y = 6t + 7.5$

11. What is the maximum value of the function $f(x) = 3\sin(x - 2) + 1$?

A) 1

B) 2

C) 3

D) 4

12. A fruit stand sells apples, bananas, and oranges at a ratio of 3:2:1. If the fruit stand sells 20 bananas, how many total pieces of fruit does the fruit stand sell?

A) 10

B) 30

C) 40

D) 60

13. The given equation represents which type of conic section?

$x^2 + 2xy + 4y^2 + 6x + 14y = 86$

A) circle

B) ellipse

C) hyperbola

D) parabola

14. A person earning a salary between $75,000 and $100,000 per year will pay $10,620 in taxes plus 20% of any amount over $75,000. What would a person earning $80,000 per year pay in taxes?

A) $10,620

B) $11,620

C) $12,120

D) $12,744

15. A bike store is having a 30%-off sale, and one of the bikes is on sale for $385. What was the original price of this bike?

A) $253.00

B) $450.00

C) $500.50

D) $550.00

16. Which expression is equivalent to $5^2 \times (-5)^{-2} - (2 + 3)^{-1}$?

A) 0

B) 1

C) $\frac{5}{4}$

D) $\frac{4}{5}$

17. Tiles are $12.51 per square yard. What will it cost to cover the floor of a room with tiles if the room is 10 feet wide and 12 feet long?

   A) $166.80

   B) $178.70

   C) $184.60

   D) $190.90

18. Jane earns $15 per hour babysitting. If she starts with $275 in her bank account, which equation represents how many hours (h) she will have to babysit for her account to reach $400?

   A) $400 = 275 + 15h$

   B) $400 = 15h$

   C) $400 = \frac{15}{h} + 275$

   D) $400 = -275 - 15h$

19. Using the information in the table, which equation demonstrates the linear relationship between x and y?

x	y
3	3
7	15
10	24

   A) $y = 6x - 6$

   B) $y = 5x - 6$

   C) $y = 4x - 6$

   D) $y = 3x - 6$

20. A chemical experiment requires that a solute be diluted with 4 parts (by mass) water for every 1 part (by mass) solute. If the desired mass for the solution is 90 grams, how many grams of solute should be used?

   A) 15 grams

   B) 16.5 grams

   C) 18 grams

   D) 22.5 grams

21. Which of the following is equivalent to $\frac{\sin x}{1 - \cos x}$?

   A) $\frac{1 + \cos x}{\sin x}$

   B) $\frac{\sin x}{\cos x}$

   C) $\tan x$

   D) 1

22. If an employee who makes $37,500 per year receives a 5.5% raise, what is the employee's new salary?

   A) $35,437.50

   B) $35,625

   C) $39,375

   D) $39,562.50

23. Which expression is equivalent to $6x + 5 \geq -15 + 8x$?

   A) $x \leq -5$

   B) $x \leq 5$

   C) $x \leq 10$

   D) $x \leq 20$

24. Juan plans to spend 25% of his workday writing a report. If he is at work for 9 hours, how many hours will he spend writing the report?

   A) 2.25

   B) 2.50

   C) 2.75

   D) 4.00

25. If a car uses 8 gallons of gas to travel 650 miles, how many miles can it travel using 12 gallons of gas?

   A) 870 miles

   B) 895 miles

   C) 915 miles

   D) 975 miles

26. If $y = 2x^2 + 12x - 3$ is written in the form $y = a(x - h)^2 + k$, what is the value of k?

A) −3

B) −15

C) −18

D) −21

27. If $f(x) = 2x^2 + 6$, what is its inverse, $f(x)^{-1}$?

A) $f(x)^{-1} = \sqrt{\dfrac{x - 6}{2}}$

B) $f(x)^{-1} = \sqrt{\dfrac{x + 6}{2}}$

C) $f(x)^{-1} = \dfrac{\sqrt{x + 6}}{2}$

D) $f(x)^{-1} = \dfrac{\sqrt{x - 6}}{2}$

28. A theater has 180 rows of seats. The first row has 10 seats. Each row has 4 seats more than the row in front of it. How many seats are in the entire theater?

A) 18,000

B) 36,200

C) 42,500

D) 66,240

29. What is the equation of the following line?

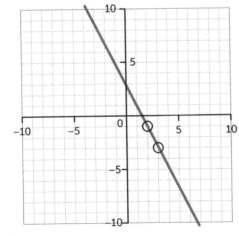

A) $y = 3x - 2$

B) $y = -3x + 2$

C) $y = 2x - 3$

D) $y = -2x + 3$

30. Which of the following graphs reflects the inequality: $3x + 6y \leq 12$?

A)
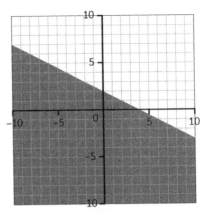

B)
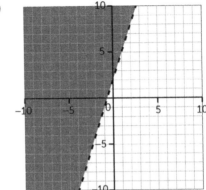

C)
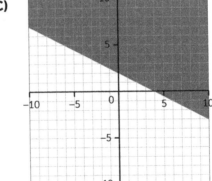

D)
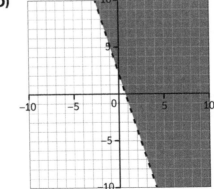

GRID-IN
Calculator

31. The graph below shows Company X's profits for the years 2010 to 2013. How much more profit did Company X make in 2013 than in 2012?

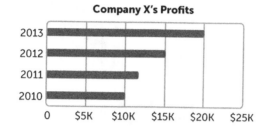

Company X's Profits

32. In 2016, LeBron James averaged 26.4 points per game over 74 games. How many points did James score that year? (Round to the nearest whole number.)

33. The circle and hexagon below both share center point T. The hexagon is entirely inscribed in the circle. The circle's radius is 5. What is the area of the shaded area?

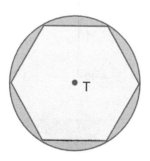

34. If a kite string is extended 10 feet and the kite is 8 feet in the air, what is the angle between the kite string and the ground?

35. Kim and Chris are writing a book together. Kim wrote twice as many pages as Chris, and together they wrote 240 pages. How many pages did Chris write?

36. The graph below shows the change in temperature from 12:00 p.m. to 6:00 p.m. At what time does the temperature begin to change the most?

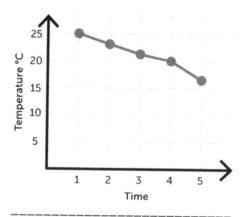

37. Fifty shares of a financial stock and 10 shares of an auto stock are valued at $1,300. If 10 shares of the financial stock and 10 shares of the auto stock are valued at $500, what is the value of 50 shares of the auto stock?

38. The average speed of cars on a highway (s) is inversely proportional to the number of cars on the road (n). If a car drives at 65 mph when there are 250 cars on the road, how fast will a car drive when there are 325 cars on the road?

Essay

Read the passages, and then write an essay based on the prompt.

As you read the passages below, consider how the writer uses:

▶ evidence, such as facts or examples, to support claims

▶ reasoning to develop ideas and to connect claims and evidence

▶ stylistic or persuasive elements, such as word choice or appeals to emotion, to add power to the ideas expressed

PASSAGE ONE

Since the hugely successful launch of Paris's Velib public bicycle share program (PBSP) in 2007, PBSPs have become a worldwide movement. Over 100 programs operate in more than 150 cities around the world, including almost fifty US cities, providing alternative transportation to millions of people. However in cities like Seattle, Washington and Melbourne, Australia, mandatory helmet laws designed to reduce injuries among bikers are stunting the growth of the system. While bikes in London and New York are typically used three to six times a day, those in Melbourne are used once at most. In 2016, Seattle's city council had to intervene when its bike program reached an unsustainably low level of participation. Even though the programs in these cities attempt to facilitate helmet access through specialized vending machines and even the availability of free helmets, mandatory helmet usage is a hurdle that deters most casual riders: the target market of PBSPs. PBSPs are a vital component of modern cities: they decrease congestion, diversify transportation options, and provide a low-cost transportation alternative for both tourists and residents. These benefits greatly outweigh the potential risk of increased injury from lack of helmet use.

PASSAGE TWO

The negative impact of mandatory helmet laws on public bicycle share programs is indisputable. However, programs that operate without such regulations pose significant public health risks. Public bicycle share systems target the casual rider who is less likely to own or carry a helmet. In systems in which helmets are available but not required, helmet usage is extremely low. Concentrated in urban areas with heavy traffic patterns, these programs encourage relatively inexperienced riders to ride in challenging conditions with insufficient protection. A study conducted by the National Institute of Health found that in cities with public bicycle share systems, head injuries increased from 42.3 percent of bicycle-related injuries before implementation of the program to 50.1 percent after implementation, and that the proportion of bicycle-related head injuries that led to admission to a trauma center increased by 14 percent. Research since the first introduction of mandatory helmet laws in the 1990s shows a consistent decrease in bicycle-related traumatic brain injuries, ranging from a decrease of 45 to 75 percent. While fewer people may use the public bikes if a mandatory helmet law in place, it is a small price to pay to ensure the safety of those who do.

PROMPT

Write an essay comparing the perspectives of the two authors. In your essay, explain how they use the techniques and elements listed above to strengthen their arguments; be sure to focus on the most relevant ones. Remember not to discuss your opinions; analyze the arguments and explain them to your audience instead.

Answer Key
READING

1. **A)** The author writes that "Owen had been remarkable for a delicate ingenuity" and that the "characteristic minuteness in his objects and accomplishments made the world even more incapable than it might otherwise have been of appreciating Owen Warland's genius."

2. **C)** In the second paragraph the author writes, "Several freaks of this kind quite destroyed the young watchmaker's credit with that steady and matter-of-fact class of people who hold the opinion that time is not to be trifled with, whether considered as the medium of advancement and prosperity in this world or preparation for the next."

3. **C)** In this sentence, "utilitarian coarseness" is contrasted with Owen's "love of the beautiful," implying that Owen has an affinity for things that are artistic and beautiful and has little interest in practical things.

4. **D)** The author writes that "the character of Owen's mind was microscopic, and tended naturally to the minute, in accordance with his diminutive frame and the marvelous smallness and delicate power of his fingers."

5. **A)** This quotation established Owen's peculiar affinity for the minute, which is reinforced by the story of his visit to the steam-engine.

6. **C)** The author writes, "Peter Hovenden's opinion of his apprentice has already been expressed. He could make nothing of the lad. Owen's apprehension of the professional mysteries, it is true, was inconceivably quick; but he altogether forgot or despised the grand object of a watchmaker's business, and cared no more for the measurement of time than if it had been merged into eternity." This implies that Peter Hovenden did not understand Owen's peculiar genius or his indifference to the measurement of time.

7. **B)** This quotation describes Peter Hovenden's opinion of Owen.

8. **B)** The author writes that "Owen's lack of sturdiness made it possible, by strict injunctions and sharp oversight, to restrain his creative eccentricity within bounds." This implies that Owen's eccentricity was unusual.

9. **A)** The author writes that "when his [Owen's] apprenticeship was served out, and he had taken the little shop which Peter Hovenden's failing eyesight compelled him to relinquish, then did people recognize how unfit a person was Owen Warland to lead old blind Father Time along his daily course."

10. **D)** The author writes that Owen's reputation in his community was "quite destroyed" as a result of his disregard for the seriousness of time.

11. **A)** Washington states that Europe is "engaged in frequent controversies" and that it would be "unwise to implicate ourselves...in the ordinary vicissitudes of her politics, or the ordinary combinations and collisions of her friendships and enmities."

12. **D)** The author writes, "It is our true policy to steer clear of permanent alliances with any portion of the foreign world; so far, I mean, as we are now at liberty to do it."

13. **A)** In this quote, Washington asserts that America should avoid foreign entanglements whenever it is possible to do so.

14. **C)** Washington asks, "Why forego the advantages of so peculiar a situation? Why quit our own to stand upon foreign ground? Why, by interweaving our destiny with that of any part of Europe, entangle our peace and prosperity in the toils of European ambition, rivalship, interest, humor, or caprice?"

15. **A)** Truman says, "To ensure the peaceful development of nations, free from coercion, the United States has taken a leading part in establishing the United Nations...We shall not realize our objectives, however, unless we are willing to help free peoples to maintain their free institutions and their national integrity against aggressive movements that seek to impose upon them totalitarian regimes."

16. **C)** The author indicates that establishing freedom from coercion means defending "free peoples...against aggressive movements that seek to impose upon them totalitarian regimes."

17. **C)** Truman states, "This was a fundamental issue in the war with Germany and Japan. Our victory was won over countries which sought to impose their will, and their way of life, upon other nations." Later, he says, "At the present moment in world history nearly every nation must choose between alternative ways of life. The choice is too often not a free one."

18. **D)** Truman states that "every nation must choose between alternative ways of life" and that "the choice is too often not a free one." He then goes on to say that "it must be the policy of the United States to support free people who are resisting attempted subjugation by armed minorities or by outside pressures."

19. **B)** Washington advocates for a policy of isolationism: "It is our true policy to steer clear of permanent alliances with any portion of the foreign world; so far, I mean, as we are now at liberty to do it." On the other hand, Truman advocates for intervention on behalf of oppressed foreign nations:"I believe that it must be the policy of the United States to support free peoples who are resisting attempted subjugation by armed minorities or by outside pressures."

20. **C)** While Washington argues that America should avoid entanglements that are "foreign to our [America's] concerns," Truman argues that any presence of "totalitarian regimes" in the world poses a threat to America's own freedom.

21. **B)** The graph indicates that there was a correlation between the new foreign policy approach and increased government spending in the twentieth century.

22. **B)** The author writes, "For centuries, philosophers have been examining the relationship between man and his social world. It is no wonder, then, that a field of study has arisen to examine just that."

23. **A)** This quote suggests that the author included Aristotle's quote in order to highlight the long-term interest in the relationship between man and his social environment.

24. **D)** The author writes that "our daily behaviors are inextricably linked with the social context in which they occur."

25. **D)** The author writes that "the behaviors we witness in others may be as much a result of social influence as they are of the individual's disposition" and that the "tendency to attribute behaviors, especially negative behaviors, to disposition is risky and can ultimately be detrimental to us and to the other person."

26. **A)** The author describes the participants as "healthy, stable, intelligent male Stanford University students" in order to provide a contrast to the "cruel and unrelenting...treatment of the prisoners."

27. **C)** The author writes, "Even giving individuals temporary power over others was enough to completely alter the way they viewed and behaved toward each other; indeed, the behaviors he witnessed in each of the groups were not a result of the dispositions of the participants but of the situation in which they had been placed."

28. **C)** The author writes that "the guards had become cruel and unrelenting in their treatment of the prisoners."

29. **C)** This quote highlights the change from the "healthy, stable, intelligent" personalities of the Stanford students and the "cruel and unrelenting" behaviors they displayed after being named guards.

30. **C)** The author writes, "Today, social psychologists study the effect of social influence on a number of different behaviors."

31. **A)** The author implies that the findings of social psychologists have practical, meaningful applications.

32. **C)** The use of the word *reconciled* indicates that scientists gathered, compared, contrasted, and integrated data into a comprehensive, global data set.

33. **B)** This quote suggests that the data was integrated into a global data set that pointed to a single conclusion about carbon fertilization.

34. C) The author writes, "Forests and other land vegetation currently remove up to 30 percent of human carbon dioxide emissions from the atmosphere during photosynthesis. If the rate of absorption were to slow down, the rate of global warming would speed up in return."

35. D) The author indicates that the research into carbon dioxide absorption "'has big implications for our understanding of whether global terrestrial ecosystems might continue to offset our carbon dioxide emissions or might begin to exacerbate climate change.'"

36. A) The author writes that climate change "decreases water availability in some regions and makes Earth warmer, leading to more frequent and larger wildfires." At the same time, those fires "stop carbon absorption by killing trees" and "spew huge amount of carbon into the atmosphere as the wood burns," contributing to the warming of Earth's atmosphere.

37. C) The author writes, "As human-caused emissions add more carbon dioxide to the atmosphere, forests worldwide are using it to grow faster, reducing the amount that stays airborne."

38. B) The author indicates that an inverse relationship exists between the rate of absorption of global forests and the rate of global warming; therefore, saving forests and increasing the rate of carbon dioxide absorption would slow the effects of climate change.

39. B) The author writes that researchers "pull[ed] together national and regional data of various kinds" to create "global data sets" that allowed them to examine carbon dioxide fertilization at many different levels.

40. D) The author writes that "Stephens used measurements of carbon dioxide made from aircraft to show that many climate models were not correctly representing flows of carbon above ground level. Models that matched the aircraft measurements better showed more carbon absorption in the tropical forests. However, there were still not enough global data sets to validate the idea of a large tropical-forest absorption."

41. D) The author writes, "Schimel noted that their paper reconciles results at every scale from the pores of a single leaf, where photosynthesis takes place, to the whole Earth, as air moves carbon dioxide around the globe."

42. B) The author writes that "many human communities want answers about the current status and future of Arctic marine mammals, including...indigenous people whose traditional ways of subsistence are intertwined with the fate of species such as ice seals, narwhals, walruses and polar bears." This implies that the survival of these groups depends on the survival of these animal species.

43. A) The author writes, "The Arctic sea ice cover...naturally grows in the fall and winter and melts during the spring and summer every year. But over the past decades, the melt season has grown longer and the average extent of Arctic sea ice has diminished."

44. **D)** The author writes that "the melt season has grown longer and the average extent of Arctic sea ice has diminished, changing the game for many Arctic marine mammals."

45. **D)** The author quotes one scientist as saying, "Mainly, just continuing daily coverage is what's important for the long-term monitoring of habitat changes."

46. **D)** The author writes that "there are many unknowns...about how their fragile habitat will evolve in a warming world." This implies that the habitat is at risk due to the changes in the earth's temperature.

47. **D)** This implies that the survival of Arctic species is in jeopardy as a result of longer melting seasons and decreased sea ice extent.

48. **D)** The author writes, "Using daily sea ice concentration data from the satellite record, he [Stern] calculated changes in the dates of the beginning of the melt season in spring and the start of the fall freeze-up from 1979 to 2013. He found that, in all regions but one, the melt season had grown longer (mostly by five to ten weeks, and by twenty weeks in one region)."

49. **A)** The author states that, unlike other Arctic species, "in the case of Arctic whales, the changes in sea ice might benefit their populations, at least in the short term: the loss and earlier retreat of sea ice opens up new habitats and, in some areas of the Arctic, has also led to an increase in food production and the length of their feeding season."

50. **C)** The author indicates that the "earlier retreat of sea ice opens up new habitats," implying the retreat of sea ice is its recession due to melting.

51. **D)** The author indicates that "monitoring" the "daily coverage" of sea ice is necessary to understanding how the expansion and recession of sea ice will shape habitats over time.

52. **C)** The graph indicates that Arctic ice extent was 8,000,000 sq. km in 1979 but is only around 2,000,000 sq. km today.

WRITING and LANGUAGE

1. **A)** This sentence effectively frames the passage's main argument: that anyone who has the required skills should consider an aerospace engineering career.

2. **C)** This choice contains an opening dash to go with the closing one following *astronautical engineering*. Also, *such as* is ungrammatical here; it is correct to delete this phrase.

3. **D)** This choice is both succinct and correctly punctuated with a semicolon. A semicolon correctly connects two related complete sentences.

4. **C)** This choice is not redundant.

5. **B)** The present-tense verb *study* agrees with the phrase *while in school*, which indicates the present tense. The modal verb *must* shows that students who want to be aerospace engineers are required to study the following topics.

6. **B)** According to the graph, the median salary for all occupations is just over eighty thousand dollars, whereas the median salary for aerospace engineers is just over one hundred thousand dollars. The difference is approximately twenty thousand dollars.

7. **A)** This sentence makes sense where it is now. The author is saying that, while aerospace engineering students must work harder in school than other engineering students must, aerospace engineers are compensated by receiving higher salaries than other engineers receive.

8. **C)** This sentence provides an effective transition between the two paragraphs. It mentions content from the fourth paragraph and then ties that in to the fifth paragraph's content.

9. **B)** The plural noun *opportunities* agrees with the plural verb *are*.

10. **D)** The relative pronoun *who* agrees with its referent, *engineers*.

11. **A)** Most people are interested in career advancement.

12. **A)** This choice is grammatical and correctly punctuated.

13. **B)** The sentence provides background information for the rest of the narrative.

14. **D)** All three verbs are in past-tense form. This agrees with most of the other verb tenses in the narrative.

15. **C)** It makes more sense that the book would be damp rather than sopping wet.

16. **A)** This detail explains why the book is damp and warped.

17. **D)** This choice shows how much effort Lincoln would put into borrowing a book.

18. **C)** Since Lincoln loves the book, he probably feels very disappointed that he will not be able to finish it. He also probably feels very guilty for ruining the borrowed book.

19. **A)** The paragraph makes good sense where it is now. It explains why Lincoln goes to the Crawford home next.

20. **B)** The relative pronoun *where* should be used to introduce the relative clause here.

21. **C)** This choice is specific enough to show that the author is referring to young Lincoln, not to Crawford.

22. **D)** Crawford asks Lincoln to work for three days; he asks that Lincoln "give [him] three days' work."

23. **C)** The singular verb *is* agrees with the singular subject *discourse*.

24. **A)** Here, *overlook* means "fail to see or take seriously."

25. **A)** The subordinating conjunction *though* correctly connects the subordinate clause to the main clause of the sentence.

26. **C)** Adding the preposition *by* creates parallel structure with the phrase *by farming and agricultural practices*.

27. **B)** Although this sentence is long, it is well constructed and properly punctuated. The reader is able to clearly understand its meaning.

28. **B)** The sentence sums up the main topic of the second paragraph, "the threat...posed...by...food production," and effectively introduces the main topic of the third paragraph, solutions to this threat.

29. **C)** The plural possessive pronoun *their* and the plural noun *careers* agree with the plural noun *researchers*, which is the sentence's subject.

30. **C)** The plural noun *lands* agrees with the plural verb *account*.

31. **A)** This sentence is well constructed and makes sense here.

32. **B)** The writer used parallel construction to write this clause; the clause includes two progressive verbs, *using* and *protecting*.

33. **B)** This sentence effectively summarizes and concludes the passage.

34. D) This sentence relates to the modern reader and effectively introduces the article's topic.

35. A) This sentence adds support for the paragraph's main point: that "creation myths are numerous and varied."

36. B) The plural phrase *these stories* agrees with its plural antecedent, *creation myths*. The singular verb *highlights* agrees with the singular noun phrase *the universal theme*.

37. B) The plural verb *were born* agrees with the plural noun *creatures*.

38. D) The phrase *in a similar manner* correctly likens man's evolution from nature to man's evolution from animals.

39. C) The sentence provides further details on early people's belief that humans evolved from coyotes.

40. B) Using a singular noun in possessive form, *humanity's*, correctly shows that the "beginning" mentioned in the sentence belongs to humanity.

41. D) The writer should use the neutral possessive pronoun *its* in this context. A rock is a thing; it is gender neutral.

42. A) This sentence mentions ancient people who "believed humans evolved from nature," the topic of the previous paragraph. It also mentions peoples who did *not* share this belief; this leads smoothly into the topic of the fifth paragraph: "stories of humanity's creation by deities."

43. C) The writer should use the object pronoun *whom* to refer to Tiamat, the god whom Marduk defeats.

44. B) The conjunction *neither* must be paired with *nor*.

MATHEMATICS: NO CALCULATOR

1. **B)** The axis of symmetry will be a vertical line that runs through the vertex, which is the point $(-3,5)$. The line of symmetry is $x = -3$.

2. **D)** Simplify using PEMDAS.

    $z^3(z + 2)^2 - 4z^3 + 2$

    $z^3(z^2 + 4z + 4) - 4z^3 + 2$

    $z^5 + 4z^4 + 4z^3 - 4z^3 + 2$

    $z^5 + 4z^4 + 2$

3. **A)** Use the points to find the slope.

    $m = \frac{y_2 - y_1}{x_2 - x_1} = \frac{-3 - 9}{4 - (-2)} = -2$

    Use the point-slope equation to find the equation of the line.

    $(y - y_1) = m(x - x_1)$

    $y - (-3) = -2(x - 4)$

    $y = -2x + 5$

4. **D)** Split the absolute value inequality into two inequalities and simplify. Switch the inequality when making one side negative.

    $\frac{x}{8} \geq 1$

    $x \geq 8$

    $-\frac{x}{8} \geq 1$

    $\frac{x}{8} \leq -1$

    $x \leq -8$

    $x \leq -8$ or $x \geq 8 \rightarrow (-\infty, -8] \cup [8, \infty)$

5. **C)** Complex solutions always come in pairs. Therefore, the number of possible complex solutions is the greatest even number equal to or less than the power of the polynomial. A 17th degree polynomial can have at most 16 complex roots.

6. **B)** Find the slope of the given line. Any parallel lines will have the same slope.

$3x + 2y = 10$

$2y = -3x + 10$

$y = -\frac{3}{2}x + 5$

7. **D)** Solve each equation for y and find the equation with a power of 1.

    $\sqrt[3]{y} = x \rightarrow y = x^3$

    $\sqrt[3]{x} = y \rightarrow y = \sqrt[3]{x}$

    $\sqrt[3]{y} = x^2 \rightarrow y = x^6$

    $y = \sqrt[3]{x^3} \rightarrow y = x$

8. **A)** His profit will be his income minus his expenses. He will earn \$40 for each lawn, or $40m$. He pays \$35 is expenses each week, or $35w$.

    profit $= 40m - 35x$

9. **B)** Factor the trinomial and set each factor equal to 0.

    $2n^2 + 2n - 12 = 0$

    $2(n^2 + n - 6) = 0$

    $2(n + 3)(n - 2) = 0$

    $n = -3$ and $n = 2$

10. **A)** The line $y = 2x + 1$ will have a slope of 2 and y-intercept of 1. The lines shown in graphs C and D have negative slopes. The line in graph B has a y-intercept of -2.

    Alternatively, use a table to find some coordinates, and identify the graph that contains those coordinates.

x	y
0	1
1	3
2	5

11. **A)** Since the cube's volume is 27, each side length is equal to $\sqrt[3]{27}$ = 3. The long diagonal distance from one of the cube's vertices to its opposite vertex will provide the sphere's diameter:

$$d = \sqrt{3^2 + 3^2 + 3^2} = \sqrt{27} = 5.2$$

Half of this length is the radius, which is **2.6 meters**.

12. **C)** Use the equation for tangent:

$$\tan 50° = \frac{x}{300}$$
$$x = 300(\tan 50°)$$

13. **A)** The domain is the possible values of x from left to right. Here, the domain starts at −4, inclusive, and stops at −1, exclusive. It starts again at 0, inclusive, and goes to 3, inclusive. The two line segments from 0 to 3 cross over each other, so the domain includes this whole interval. Note that closed circles represent inclusion (square bracket), and open circles represent exclusions (round bracket).

14. **C)** Only II and III define y as a function of x.

I. This is not a function: the equation represents a horizontal parabola, which fails the vertical line test.

II. This is a function: each x-value corresponds to only one y-value.

III. This is a function: the graph passes the vertical line test.

15. **D)** Find where the denominator equals 0.

$$-2x - 6 = 0$$
$$\boldsymbol{x = -3}$$

16. The slope of a horizontal line is always **0**.

17. Isolate the $\sqrt{2x - 5}$ by subtracting 4:

$$\sqrt{2x - 5} = x - 4$$

Square both sides to clear the radical:

$$2x - 5 = x^2 - 8x + 16$$

Collect all variables to one side:

$$x^2 - 10x + 21 = 0$$

Factor and solve.

$$(x - 7)(x - 3) = 0$$
$$x = 7 \text{ or } x = 3$$

Check solutions by plugging into the original, as squaring both sides can cause extraneous solutions:

$$\sqrt{2(3) - 5} + 4 = 3$$
$$\sqrt{1} + 4 = 3$$

False, 3 is NOT a solution.

$$\sqrt{2(7) - 5} + 4 = 7$$
$$\sqrt{9} + 4 = 7$$

True, 7 is a solution.

$$\boldsymbol{X = 7}$$

18. The given values can be used to write two equations for the area of $\triangle WXZ$ with two sets of bases and heights. First, determine the quantities known and the quantity needed:

$$WZ = b_1 = 80$$
$$XU = h_1 = 70$$
$$XZ = b_2 = 100$$
$$WY = h_2 = ?$$

Next, use the formula for the area of a triangle to find the unknown quantity:

$$A = \frac{1}{2}bh$$
$$A_1 = \frac{1}{2}(80)(70) = 2800$$

$A_2 = \frac{1}{2}(100)(h_2)$

Set the two equations equal to each other, and solve for WY.

$2800 = \frac{1}{2}(100)(h_2)$

$h_2 = 56$

WY = 56

19. Plug 0 in for x and solve for y.

$7y - 42x + 7 = 0$

$7y - 42(0) + 7 = 0$

$y = -1$

The y-intercept is at (0,−1).

20. Rewrite the bases so they are the same, then set the exponents equal and solve.

$16x + 10 = 83x$

$(24)x + 10 = (23)3x$

$24x + 40 = 29x$

$4x + 40 = 9x$

$40 = 9x - 4x$

$40 = 5x$

x = 8

MATHEMATICS: CALCULATOR

1. **C)** Use the formula for percentages.

$percent = \dfrac{part}{whole}$

$= \dfrac{42}{48}$

$= 0.875 = $ **87.5%**

2. **C)** Use the formula for percent change.

$percent\ change = \dfrac{amount\ of\ change}{original\ amount}$

$= \dfrac{7,375 - 7,250}{7,250} = 0.017 = $ **1.7%**

3. **D)** Factor the equation and set each factor equal to 0.

$y = 16x^3 - 48x^2$

$16x^2(x - 3) = 0$

x = 0 and x = 3

4. **C)** Set up a system of equations where d equals the number of dimes and q equals number of quarters.

$d + q = 34$

$0.1d + 0.25q = 6.25$

$0.1d + 0.25(34 - d) = 6.25$

$d = 15$

$q = 34 - 15 = $ **19**

5. **D)** Plug in each set of values and determine if the inequality is true.

$2(0) + 0 \leq -10$ FALSE

$2(10) + 2 \leq -10$ FALSE

$2(10) + 10 \leq -10$ FALSE

2(−10) + (−10) ≤ −10 TRUE

6. **C)** One way to find the answer is to draw a picture.

Put 24 cans into groups of 4. One out of every 4 cans is diet (light gray) so there is 1 light gray can for every 3 dark gray cans. That leaves 18 dark gray cans (regular soda).

Alternatively, solve the problem using ratios.

$\dfrac{regular}{total} = \dfrac{3}{4} = \dfrac{x}{24}$

$4x = 72$

x = 18

7. **D)** The surface area will be the area of the square base plus the area of the four triangles. First, find the area of the square ($A = s^2$; $6^2 = 36$). Then, to find the area of the triangles, first find the pyramid's slant height:

$c^2 = a^2 + b^2$

$l^2 = 100 + 9$

$l = \sqrt{109}$

Find the area of the triangle face using the slant height as the height of the triangle face:

$A = \frac{1}{2}bh$

$A = \frac{1}{2}(6)(\sqrt{109})$

$A = 3\sqrt{109}$

Finally, add the area of the square base and the four triangles to find the total surface area:

$SA = 36 + 4(3\sqrt{109})$

$SA \approx \textbf{161.3 cm}$

8. **D)** Identify the important parts of the circle.

$r = 3$

length of $\overline{ACB} = 5$

Plug these values into the formula for the length of an arc and solve for θ.

$s = \frac{\theta}{360°} \times 2\pi r$

$5 = \frac{\theta}{360} \times 2\pi(3)$

$\frac{5}{6\pi} = \frac{\theta}{360}$

$\theta = 95.5°$

$m\angle AOB = \textbf{95.5°}$

9. **C)** Use the formula for percent change.

percent change $= \dfrac{\text{amount of change}}{\text{original amount}}$

$= \dfrac{(680 - 425)}{425}$

$= \dfrac{255}{425} = 0.60 = \textbf{60\%}$

10. **B)** There are 16 ounces in a pound, so the baby's starting weight is 120 ounces. He gained 6 ounces per month, or $6t$. So, the baby's weight will be his initial weight plus the amount gained for each month:

$y = \textbf{6}t + \textbf{120}$

11. **D)** This sine function has an amplitude of 3 and has been shifted up 1, so it has a **maximum value of 4**.

12. **D)** Assign variables and write the ratios as fractions. Then, cross-multiply to solve for the number of apples and oranges sold.

$x = $ apples

$\dfrac{\text{apples}}{\text{bananas}} = \dfrac{3}{2} = \dfrac{x}{20}$

$60 = 2x$

$x = 30$ apples

$y = $ oranges

$\dfrac{\text{oranges}}{\text{bananas}} = \dfrac{1}{2} = \dfrac{y}{20}$

$2y = 20$

$y = 10$ oranges

To find the total, add the number of apples, oranges, and bananas together. $30 + 20 + 10 = \textbf{60 pieces of fruit}$.

13. **B)** Calculate the discriminant.

$B^2 - 4AC = 2^2 - 4(1)(4) = -12$

The discriminant is negative and A $\neq$ C, so **it is an ellipse**.

14. **B)** Add the base amount and the tax on the extra percentage of the person's income.

$10,620 + 0.2(80,000 - 75,000)$

$= \textbf{\$11,620}$

15. **D)** Set up an equation. The original price (p) minus 30% of the original price is \$385.

$p - 0.3p = 385$

$p = \dfrac{385}{0.7} = \textbf{\$550}$

16. **D)** Simplify using PEMDAS.

$5^2 \times (-5)^{-2} - 5^{-1}$

$= 25 \times \dfrac{1}{25} - \dfrac{1}{5}$

$= 1 - \dfrac{1}{5} = \dfrac{\textbf{4}}{\textbf{5}}$

17. A) Find the area of the room in square feet and convert it to square yards (1 square yard = 9 square feet). Then multiply by the cost per square yard.

area = 10 × 12 = 120 square feet

$\frac{120}{9} = \frac{40}{3}$ square yards

$\frac{40}{3}$ × \$12.51 = $\frac{\$500.40}{3}$

=\$166.80

18. A) The amount of money in Jane's bank account can be represented by the expression $275 + 15h$ (\$275 plus \$15 for every hour she works). Therefore, the equation **$400 = 275 + 15h$** describes how many hours she needs to babysit to have \$400.

19. D) Substitute one (x,y) pair into each answer choice to find the correct equation.

A) $y = 6x - 6$; (3,3)

$y = 6(3) - 6$

$y = 18 - 6$

$y = 12 \neq 3$

B) $y = 5x - 6$; (3,3)

$y = 5(3) - 6$

$y = 15 - 6$

$y = 9 \neq 3$

C) $y = 4x - 6$; (3,3)

$y = 4(3) - 6$

$y = 12 - 6$

$y = 6 \neq 3$

D) $y = 3x - 6$; (3,3)

$y = 3(3) - 6$

$y = 9 - 6$

$y = 3$

20. C) The ratio of solute to solution is 1:5. Write a proportion and solve.

$\frac{1}{5} = \frac{x}{90}$

$1(90) = x(5)$

$18 = x$

21. A) Use trigonometric identities.

$\frac{\sin x}{1 - \cos x} \times \frac{1 + \cos x}{1 + \cos x}$

$\frac{(\sin x)(1 + \cos x)}{1 - \cos^2 x}$

$\frac{(\sin x)(1 + \cos x)}{\sin^2 x}$

$\frac{1 + \cos x}{\sin x}$

22. D) Find the amount of change and add to the original amount.

amount of change = original amount × percent change

= 37,500 × 0.055 = 2,062.50

37,500 + 2,062.50 = **\$39,562.50**

23. C) Isolate the variable on the left side of the inequality. Reverse the direction of the inequality when dividing by a negative number.

$6x + 5 \geq -15 + 8x$

$-2x + 5 \geq -15$

$-2x \geq -20$

$x \leq 10$

24. A) Use the equation for percentages.

part = whole × percentage = 9 × 0.25 = **2.25**

25. D) Set up a proportion and solve.

$\frac{8}{650} = \frac{12}{x}$

$12(650) = 8x$

$x = 975$ miles

26. D) Complete the square to put the quadratic equation in vertex form.

$y = 2x^2 + 12x - 3$

$y = 2(x^2 + 6x + \underline{\quad}) - 3 + \underline{\quad}$

$y = 2(x^2 + 6x + 9) - 3 - 18$

$y = 2(x + 3)^2 - 21$

27. **A)** Swap x and y in the equation, then solve for y.

$f(x) = 2x^2 + 6$

$y = 2x^2 + 6$

$x = 2y^2 + 6$

$$y = \sqrt{\frac{(x-6)}{2}}$$

28. **D)** Use the formula for the sum of an arithmetic series.

$S_n = \frac{n}{2}(a_1 + a_n)$

$= \frac{n}{2}[2a_1 + (n-1)d]$

$= \frac{180}{2}[2(10) + (180-1)4]$

$= \textbf{66,240 seats}$

29. **D)** The y-intercept can be identified on the graph as $(0,3)$, so $b = 3$. To find the slope, choose any two points and plug the values into the slope equation. The two points chosen here are $(2,-1)$ and $(3,-3)$:

$m = \frac{(-3)-(-1)}{3-2} = \frac{-2}{1} = -2$

Replace m with -2 and b with 3 in $y = mx + b$.

$\textbf{y = -2x + 3}$

30. **A)** The x- and y-intercepts are $(4,0)$ and $(0,2)$. Because of the inequality, the graph must be shaded below the line, making A) the correct choice.

$3x + 6y \leq 12$

$3(0) + 6y = 12$

$y = 2$

y-intercept: $(0,2)$

$3x + 6(0) \leq 12$

$x = 4$

x-intercept: $(4,0)$

31. **$5,000**

Find Company X's profits for 2012 and 2013 from the bar graph:

2012 profit ≈ $15,000

2013 profit ≈ $20,000

Subtract to find the change in profit:

$20,000 − $15,000 = **$5,000**

32. Multiply the average number of points per game by the number of games he played:

26.4 × 74 = 1953.6 ≈ **1954 points**

33. The area of the shaded region will be the area of the circle minus the area of the hexagon. Use the radius to find the area of the circle.

$AC = \pi r^2$

$= \pi(5)^2$

$= 25\pi$

To find the area of the hexagon, draw a right triangle from the vertex, and use special right triangles to find the hexagon's apothem. Then, use the apothem to calculate the area.

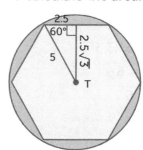

$a = 2.5\sqrt{3}$

$A_H = \frac{ap}{2}$

$= \frac{(2.5\sqrt{3})(30)}{2}$

$= 64.95$

Subtract the area of the hexagon from the circle to find the area of the shaded region.

$= A_C - A_H$

$= 25\pi - 64.95$

$≈ \textbf{13.55}$

34. Use trigonometry and a diagram to solve. The scenario can be represented by this diagram:

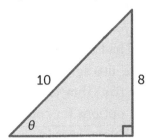

Write an equation that relates angle θ to the opposite side and the hypotenuse.

$\sin\theta = \dfrac{8}{10}$

Use the inverse of sine to solve for the angle.

$\theta = \sin^{-1}\dfrac{8}{10} = \mathbf{53°}$

35. Write a formula to find the answer.

p = number of pages written by Chris

$2p$ = number of pages written by Kim

$p + 2p = 240$

$p = 80$

Chris wrote 80 pages.

36. 4:00 p.m.

At 4:00 p.m., the temperature started to change the most, dropping rapidly from 4 to 5 p.m. This can be determined by subtracting the temperature values from 4:00 p.m. and 5:00 p.m., or by observing that the line connecting the values at 4 and 5 is the steepest on the graph.

37. Set up a system of equations and solve using elimination.

f = the cost of a financial stock

a = the cost of an auto stock

$50f + 10a = 1300$

$10f + 10a = 500$

$50f + 10a = 1300$

$\underline{+\ -50f - 50a = -2500}$

$-40a = -1{,}200$

$a = 30$

$50(30) = \mathbf{1{,}500}$

38. Use the formula for inversely proportional relationships to find k and then solve for s.

$sn = k$

$(65)(250) = k$

$k = 16{,}250$

$s(325) = 16{,}250$

$\boldsymbol{s = 50}$

SAMPLE ESSAY

As public bicycle share programs (PBSPs) increase in popularity, significant debate has emerged over helmet requirements in cities that implement these systems. Both sides of the debate agree that helmets improve safety for bicycle riders. Historically, mandatory bicycle laws have greatly increased helmet usage and had a significant impact on reducing traumatic brain injuries. Both sides of the debate also agree that PBSPs provide both transportation and environmental benefits to cities. They can decrease congestion and provide low-cost and flexible transportation options for commuters and tourists. Finally, both perspectives agree that mandatory helmet laws hamper the development of bicycle-based urban public transportation, by discouraging riders from partaking in the system. The conflict between the two camps centers on how cities should balance their responsibility to individual safety and public policy goals.

Cities with mandatory helmet laws have struggled to get their programs off the ground, experiencing significantly decreased participation rates. For example, according to Passage 1, Melbourne, which has a mandatory helmet law, has a participation rate anywhere from 67 to 83 percent lower than London, which has no such law. Without extensive participation, the societal benefits of PBSPs are greatly diminished. While Melbourne's system still offers a transportation alternative, it is clearly not viewed as a viable one by most of the population, and so provides little benefit in that way. Also, with such markedly low participation rates, impact on congestion and pollution would be negligible.

On the other hand, PBSP riders typically do not have extensive experience riding in urban environments whose increased traffic can pose greater risk of an accident. According to Passage 2, a recent study shows that PBSPs that do not mandate helmets increase the chance of a rider suffering a traumatic brain injury during a biking accident. This increase could potentially create new policy problems as it impacts one of the city government's primary goals: ensuring the safety of its people.

Some cities have attempted to make helmets more accessible by installing helmet vending machines near bike stations or even leaving free helmets out for riders, according to Passage 1. However, according to Passage 2, few people take advantage of these options. This indicates that people would rather opt out than use a helmet; perhaps issues beyond accessibility factor into the equation. For example, while people are willing to share bicycles, they may not be willing to share headgear, which could be perceived as unsanitary. Or riders could be concerned with fitting, as helmets come in a variety of sizes. The nature of PBSPs can also be a factor. The majority of PBSP users are casual riders according to Passage 1, who are attracted by the flexibility and ease of use the programs. This includes tourists or commuters who perhaps did not even intend to ride a bike when they set out. Even if it does not actually require any increased effort, such users may simply feel that helmet laws detract from the open nature of PBSPs.

Because both sides of the debate agree that helmet usage is preferable and that PBSPs are beneficial, several questions on this topic are open to further research.

For example, researchers should examine the overall number of injuries in cities with PBSPs compared to those without, and how the volume of users impacts both rider and vehicle safety on the road. They could also look at how the modification of roads to accommodate bikers by installing protected bike lanes, for example, impacts safety numbers. Finally, researchers could explore alternative ways to encourage helmet use beyond legislation.

To take your SECOND SAT practice test, follow the link below:

www.acceptedinc.com/sat-2020-online-resources

Made in the USA
Middletown, DE
17 August 2023

36827564R10110